WATER RESOURCES MANAGEMENT SERIES: 5

Core and Periphery: A Comprehensive Approach to Middle Eastern Water

Water Resources Management Series

General Editor: Asit K. Biswas (Oxford, UK)
Editorial Board: Mahmoud A. Abu-Zeid (Cairo, Egypt)
Madhav A. Chitale (New Delhi, India)
Aly M. Shady (Ottawa, Canada)
Malin Falkenmark (Sweden)

1. *Water for Sustainable Development in the Twenty-first Century*, edited by ASIT K. BISWAS, MOHAMMED JELLAL and GLENN STOUT
2. *International Waters of Middle East: From Euphrates-Tigris to Nile*, edited by ASIT K. BISWAS
3. *Management and Development of Major Rivers*, edited by ALY M. SHADY, MOHAMED EL-MOATTASSEM, ESSAM ALY ABDEL-HAFIZ and ASIT K. BISWAS
4. *Asian International Waters*, edited by ASIT K. BISWAS and TSUYOSHI HASHIMOTO

WATER RESOURCES MANAGEMENT SERIES: 5

Core and Periphery: A Comprehensive Approach to Middle Eastern Water

By

ASIT K. BISWAS (Chairman)
JOHN KOLARS
MASAHIRO MURAKAMI
JOHN WATERBURY
AARON WOLF
Members, Middle East Water Commission

Sponsored by
Middle East Water Commission
With the support of
Sasakawa Peace Foundation

DELHI
OXFORD UNIVERSITY PRESS
CALCUTTA CHENNAI MUMBAI
1997

Oxford University Press, Walton Street, Oxford OX2 6DP

Oxford New York
Athens Auckland Bangkok Calcutta
Cape Town Chennai Dar es Salaam Delhi
Florence Hong Kong Istanbul Karachi
Kuala Lumpu Madrid Melbourne Mexico City
Mumbai Nairobi Paris Singapore
Taipei Tokyo Toronto

and associates in

Berlin Ibadan

ISBN 0 19 564062 4

Typeset at Print Line, New Delhi 110048
Printed in India at Rekha Printers Pvt. Ltd., New Delhi 110020
and published by Manzar Khan, Oxford University Press
YMCA Library Building, Jai Singh Road, New Delhi 110 001

This book is dedicated to

Akira Iriyama and Takashi Shirasu

*President and Chief Programme Officer
Sasakawa Peace Foundation
without whose support and encouragement
this book could never have been written*

Foreword

In the summer of 1991, Professor Asit K. Biswas, the then President of the International Water Resources Association and Senior Scientific Advisor to the Executive Director of the United Nations Environment Programme, visited the Sasakawa Peace Foundation in Tokyo, to discuss possible areas of collaboration with Dr Takashi Shirasu, the Chief Programme Officer of our Foundation. One of the main items of their discussion was a new initiative to promote regional cooperation in the Middle East in the area of water resources by fostering a dialogue between the key players of the countries and major international institutions concerned. It was felt that a new negotiating mechanism could be effectively used, under the aegis of a nongovernmental organization, through which many of the most contentious problems associated with the current regional water use and management problems of the Middle East could be resolved. It would be a parallel track event to the continuing bilateral and multilateral talks between the countries concerned, where by that time actual progress on the difficult issues concerned was very limited and painfully slow.

The discussion between Dr Biswas and Dr Shirasu led to the eventual agreement to organize a Middle East Water Forum to review and discuss the principal water issues of the area in Cairo, Egypt, 7–9 February 1993. It was believed that if the Forum was carefully planned and properly organized, it could significantly facilitate the bilateral and multilateral negotiations between the countries concerned by identifying various feasible alternative scenarios for resolving the long-smouldering historical problems which the countries of the region had to face due to serious shortages of water availability, combined with steadily increasing demands. It was also felt that a free and informal dialogue between the main inter-country negotiators of the water issue, without the presence of the media and the general public, could also be considered as an important confidence-building measure, which could accelerate, or even reinforce, formal diplomatic initiatives in this area.

The Sasakawa Peace Foundation thus joined hands with the United Nations Environment Programme (UNEP) and the United Nations University (UNU) to support the International Water Resources Association (IWRA) to convene the Middle East Water Forum. In retrospect, we were very fortunate that Professor Biswas personally took charge of convening the Forum. He has been directly involved with the various Middle East water issues for more than three decades, and during this period he has advised most of the governments of the region and all the international organizations on such issues officially at very high levels. Furthermore, his expertise on water management has been well-acknowledged internationally, and his objectivity and impartiality in water issues of the region are unquestionable. He is thus equally acceptable to all the parties concerned.

The participation to the Forum was by invitation only. Twenty-seven participants to the Forum were carefully chosen, and it is indeed remarkable that all the experts invited by Professor Biswas in their personal capacities, promptly agreed to take part. Seventeen of the participants were directly involved in bilateral and multilateral Peace Talks.

By all accounts, the Forum was an outstanding success. It turned out to be a remarkable exercise in international relations and preventive diplomacy. The book that was subsequently published by Oxford University Press containing all the specially commissioned papers for the Forum, *International Waters of the Middle East: From Euphrates-Tigris to Nile*, is now considered to be the most definitive text available on the subject.

Following the Forum and during one of his very regular visits to Japan, Professor Biswas and Dr Shirasu discussed how best to follow up the most remarkable results that were produced by the Forum. It was agreed that a Middle East Water Commission should be established, with a fixed set of objectives and a limited lifespan of three years. The Foundation agreed to support the Commission, and Professor Biswas agreed to chair it personally.

After a great deal of discussion and deliberation, it was decided that no member of the Commission should be from any of the countries of the region, but rather well-known experts on the water problems of the region, who are equally acceptable to all the countries concerned. It was felt that if any one member of the Commission came from one of the countries of the region, other countries would have to be represented as well. This would not only transform the Commission into a 'mini United Nations', but also a large membership would make its functioning somewhat inefficient. Equally, past experiences indicated that the commissions with large memberships have seldom produced worthwhile and innovative results, since their reports are invariably full of compromises that are acceptable to each and every one of their many members.

In addition to Professor Biswas, other members of the Commission were Professor John Kolars (University of Michigan), Dr Masahiro Murakami (Nippon Koei, Japan), Professor John Waterbury (Princeton University) and Professor Aaron Wolf (University of Alabama).

The Commission first met in 28-30 September, 1993 in Santa Fe, USA, during which a detailed work programme was prepared. In the summer of 1994, all the Commission members spent a month at Princeton University to prepare a preliminary draft. In late 1994, during the World Water Congress in Cairo, the Commission outlined its preliminary findings and views. The Cairo Congress was attended by more than 600 water specialists from around sixty-three countries, including a large number of participants from the Middle East. A lively interchange took place between the Commission members and a packed audience. In August 1995, the Commission was specially invited to outline its findings at the Stockholm Water Symposium, the premier international water event each year. The final meeting of the Commission took place in Ankara, Turkey, 1–2 February 1996.

During the entire working life of the Commission, it kept regular contacts with all the governments of the region, as well as with other interested governments and international organizations who were actively promoting peace in the region. Among the latter were. Canada, Japan, United States, UNDP, and the World Bank. Professor Biswas not only directed the substantive work of the Commission, but also during his 'normal' course of work as an advisor to seventeen governments and all the major international organizations at the senior-most levels, he used his extensive network and personal contacts to keep up a continual dialogue with all the major players of the

Middle East water issues. Furthermore, all the other Commission members equally used their own individual networks to keep numerous other people informed.

The Commission has published numerous papers in major international journals during the past three years. All these carefully planned activities mean that this has been one of the very few commissions ever established which has ensured regular dialogues with all the interested parties throughout its entire life.

The Sasakawa Peace Foundation is indeed most grateful to the Commission members, Professor Kolars, Dr Murakami, Professor Waterbury and Prof. Wolf, and especially to its Chairman, Professor Biswas, for their excellent work in the complex and difficult hydropolitical issues of the Middle East. Their hard work has already contributed to many significant positive developments in the region. The publication of the present report will no doubt further add to the accomplishments of the Commission. In addition, the many seeds the Commission has sown in terms of new and innovative ideas and through the creation of numerous informal networks, will further add to its achievements.

The Sasakawa Peace Foundation is proud to have played a key role in the establishment of the Middle East Water Commission and its overall functioning. It has been one of our most successful projects. Since no lasting peace in the Middle East will ever be possible without a just and rational agreement on the use and management of its meagre water resources, we sincerely hope that the work of the Commission will play an important role in bringing permanent peace to the region, and will contribute to significant prosperity to all the countries concerned on a sustainable basis.

Akira Iriyama
President
Sasakawa Peace Foundation
Tokyo, Japan

Contents

Figures and Tables

Preface

Water has always been a scarce resource in the arid countries of the Middle East, where one of the main constraints to development has been water, not land. However, as the population of the countries has steadily increased, both due to natural causes and migration, the situation has progressively worsened in terms of availability of adequate quantity and quality of water. All the current indicators point to the fact that the problems are most likely to worsen even further in the coming years, unless radical changes can be made in its overall management in the foreseeable future.

No sane individual will argue with the fact that lasting peace in the Middle East is not possible without a satisfactory resolution of the main problems associated with water between the countries concerned. While the problems are complex, and the available solutions may not be easily implemented due to a variety of interrelated social, economic, technical, institutional and political problems, both within the individual countries as well as between the countries, the fact remains that, given good will and political will from all sides, the water problems of the Middle East are solvable. It will certainly require enlightened leadership in the countries and strong political commitment to the solutions, but, as the present report of the Middle East Water Commission indicates, there are solutions.

The events of the past few years indicate that there are good reasons to be very cautiously optimistic that the water problems of the region could be resolved some time in the future. There is no doubt that mutually acceptable solutions would take time to surface, and equally the process to reach them would not be linear. There would be reasons for optimism as well as pessimism all along the way until hard and realistic decisions can be taken by the countries leaders and accepted by the majority of their citizens.

Water has become an integral component of the ongoing peace process for the region. As the various negotiations have progressed, and some bilateral treaties signed, there is more reason for muted optimism now compared to even five or ten years ago. The fact is that, for the most part, parties are meeting each other, officially or unofficially, individually or collectively; new approaches to water acquisition and equitable sharing are under active discussion, regionally and internationally; and possible technological solutions to the growing water scarcities are being carefully studied and some are being gradually put in place. These are positive developments. They can be considered as good omens for the future. In any event, alternatives to the possible solutions are not difficult to contemplate; these can only result in untold misery for the people of the region for many years to come.

When I convened the Middle East Water Forum in Cairo in February 1993, with the support of the Sasakawa Peace Foundation and the United Nations Environment Programme, one of our main objectives was to bring some of the key players of the countries of the region and major international organizations to discuss the various complex and interrelated issues in an informal atmosphere. The success of the Forum led to the establishment of the Middle East Water Commission. Mr Akira Inyama, President of the Sasakawa Peace Foundation, has succinctly outlined the background to the establishment of this Commission in his Foreward to this book. (They will not be repeated here.)

Chairing the Commission has been a challenging experience. When I accepted the Chairmanship, and because I have known the region well for some twenty-five years, I fully expected the task to be difficult and complex, but intellectually rewarding. In retrospect, overall, the task was more or less what I had anticipated, even though some problems turned out more complex than initially foreseen, and others less so.

Many people, both from the Middle East region and outside, have assisted the Commission in our work, for which we are truly grateful. Without their unstinted help and sound advice, we simply could not have achieved what we managed. Because of the sensitive nature of the issues and the large number of individuals and institutions that have assisted us, no names are being mentioned here. However, without their assistance, their report and all of our other associated activities simply would not have been possible. Our most sincere appreciation goes to each one of them.

The main strength of any Commission, however, comes from its members. I was most fortunate in having some of the best specialists anywhere in the world, on the Middle East water issue, as members of the Commission. They represented different disciplines, and our knowledge and expertise of the region complemented each other remarkably well. In addition, it was a real pleasure and privilege for me to work with each of them intensively and extensively. I am thus most grateful to Professor John Kolars, Dr Masahiro Murakami, Professor John Waterbury and Professor Aaron Wolf for their excellent work as members of the Commission and the outstanding way they performed their individual tasks. Their unrivalled knowledge of the region and objective analyses of the complex issues have been some of the primary causes of the success of the Commission.

Last but no least I wish to express my personal gratitude and appreciation to Dr Takashi Shirasu of the Sasakawa Peace Foundation, Tokyo, His wise counsel and regular encouragement was a source of continuous inspiration to me. He took a genuine personal interest in our work, and we have all benefited because of it. Without his help, the Commission would not have been able to achieve even half of what it did.

Even though the work of the Commission is now complete, members of the Commission will continue to be active in the Middle East water issues in the years ahead. As Chairman of the Commission, I sincerely hope that our work, in some measurable ways, will contribute to the satisfactory resolution of Middle East water issues in the future.

Asit K. Biswas
Middle East Water Commission
Instituto de Ingeniería
Universidad Nacional Autónoma de México,
México, D.F., México

Part I

The Parameters of Water Project Development in the Middle East

1 Thoughts on the Predictability, Reliability, and Costs of Water in the Middle East

INTRODUCTION

A sense of immediacy has influenced peace negotiators in the Middle East. Hostilities and the angst they bring must cease; the window of opportunity must not be missed! The accords between Israel and Jordan and between Israel and Palestine[1] in 1995 seemed impossible only months before. Accompanying such political rapprochements have been parallel efforts to solve the problems of water sharing among the participants. It is in this spirit that such confidence building measures as the completion, in September 1995, of a canal from the Sea of Galilee to the East Ghor canal, which will deliver 50 mcm potable water annually to Jordan, have taken place. The Red-Dead canal and small storage dams on the Jordan also have been proposed for the near future and their feasibility is being studied. Nevertheless, the urgency of time and politics often compel other vital parameters of the regional water situation to be overlooked.

We must not forget that it is an enduring peace which is sought, a peace which must hold not for the moment but indefinitely. Such a peace must include considerations of water supply which can survive pressure from growing populations, wide and unpredictable fluctuations in regional climate, and unforeseen political swings. We disagree with those who tend to downgrade the importance of water in the regional peace process. Our own belief is that the water issue is a necessary though not a sufficient feature of regional co-operation.

Others have discussed the continuing and growing need for water in the Middle East and have painted a broad picture of the priorities involved (Rogers, 1994, Chapter 11). Such efforts describe in general terms the problems faced in satisfying future thirst and their possible solutions, but as is said, 'the devil is in the details'. We hope to exorcise some of these details in the pages ahead. Our purpose is to suggest a more specific blueprint for the hydro-development of the Jordan river basin and the area which surrounds it. We also intend to extend the planning horizon far enough into the future to consider the possibility of importing water from outside the region.

A detailed look at the region's climate, demography, and economy indicates that no single water project, nor narrowly focused combination of such projects, can serve its future inhabitants. At the same time, increases in population will place additional pressures upon existing supplies. Water-related technologies which determine the expense with which such supplies are obtained will continue to change. So, too, will local supplies of brackish and fresh water vary as old sources are depleted and polluted and new sources become available through improved means of purification and pumping.

This is an attempt to provide a region-wide review of water issues and technologies and to show how they can be welded sequentially into a long-term, integrated system which will serve all the people of the region, not only now but in the future. We do not espouse any particular project or water source, but hope to demonstrate how various approaches when combined will serve the region best.

PARAMETERS OF WATER AVAILABILITY

Water seldom is directly available to the consumer at its source. Water becomes available for consumption only after passing through a complex of natural, social and financial filters. The focus of this discussion is the Jordan river basin and the problems of water supply for its growing populations. This area becomes the core of the study, but does not constitute its geographical limits. Beyond the core are sources of water which may become available to the core through human means. These constitute the periphery.

While the present Middle East water crisis centres upon Israel, Jordan, and Palestine (the West Bank and Gaza), that is the core area, Syria and Lebanon, at somewhat greater remove, are also involved. Turkey and Iraq are even more peripheral but assume importance as the time span under consideration increases. Egypt and the Nile and the Arabian peninsula must also be taken into consideration despite their unique sets of water-related problems. One might possibly think of such matters in terms of the length of time it would take a unit of water to flow to Amman or Gaza from a well located nearby or through a pipeline from distant mountains. Thus, the concept of core and periphery should be viewed not only in a spatial but also in a synchronous temporal context.

The complex of variables referred to above may also be considered in terms of different rates of change over time, i.e., a diachronous view and Fig. 1-1 illustrates this point. The variables affecting water delivery are grouped according to the basic conditions which determine their impact upon availability: that is, predictability, reliability, and cost.

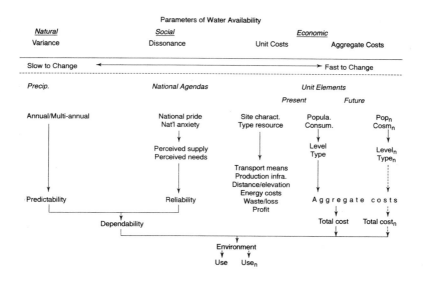

Fig. 1-1: Parameters of Water Availability

Our reasoning is thus: By predictability is meant the variance of a given phenomenon. Annual and multi-annual variance of precipitation are listed under this heading. The uncontested rule relating to precipitation variance is 'the more sparse the rainfall, the more uncertain it becomes as to amount, time, or location'. Unpredictability, the nemesis of agricultural planners and water managers is of particular importance in the core of the study area (Bakour and Kolars). To the south of the core (excluding the valley of the Nile) the deserts of the Arabian peninsula and North Africa are predictably arid; to its north, the rain-fed lands of Turkey enjoy a more certain climatic regime than do those of the core. World and regional climatic patterns are slow to change, and though it may seem cold comfort to those concerned, the unpredictability of precipitation in the core is a certainty and can be expected to remain predictably so within the limits of any planning period.

Slowest to change are those debatable and imperfectly perceived variables such as global warming and climatic change. Among those quickest to change, and also simplest to quantify, are the engineering and investment costs involved in supplying water. These are expressed by the per unit price and the aggregate cost of water which reflects the size and characteristics of the consumer population.

The per unit price of water is tied to a number of natural and technological factors as well as to the producer's desire for profit. Sources (springs, rivers, aquifers) and site characteristics are primary in these considerations. For example, is the water to be desalinized brackish or sea water? Significant differences in cost stem from this. Is the reservoir site in a deep canyon or on an undulating plain? Water loss through evaporation, plus major differences in dam construction apply here. The means of transfer also influence ultimate cost. If pipelines, how far between source and consumer, and what are the costs of pumping and lifting the water? What waste and loss will occur? The type of production facility plays its role: desalination plant or high dam? What energy costs are involved in reverse osmosis—is hydro-power involved? Or is imported fuel for a thermal plant a concern? Finally, what will the producer and shipper consider to be a reasonable per unit profit? It should be noted that the time horizon for these costs may vary, but all fall within the scope of a few years and are tied to the market mechanism. Therefore, this group of variables has been placed near the 'quick to change' end of the continuum.

When per unit water costs are aggregated in terms of the consuming population not only the size but the projected growth rates are important, as are the level and type of consumption. These measures lead to consideration of even more complex variables that often create social dissonance related to the national agendas of the peoples involved.

The fact that feelings seemingly elude quantification does not preclude consideration of their role in water availability. This parameter is discussed in Chapter 5 where Coplin and O'Leary's PRINCE Political Accounting System is considered. A few instances of how politics and emotions intersect will suffice at this juncture. International relations can be good or poor, and the perceptions that one nation's population has of another's can also play an important role. National pride which may insist upon the internal production of a resource regardless of its cost is frequently encountered as is national anxiety. The familiar question of food security couched in terms of water availability and security needs little explication. The perception of need and the perception of supply also can be part of the national *Zeitgeist*. Is a nation like Saudi Arabia, which some say is graced with 'Forty Niles beneath its sands', being realistic regarding the future of its water supply? Does such a quantity of water really exist there? And what of Israeli swimming pools and golf courses against an adequate per capita supply of safe drinking water in Gaza? Attitudes and perceptions do change, but more slowly than the size of populations or the stock market. On the other hand the juggernaut like pace of possible global climatic change is slower than the tides of human affairs. In Fig. 1-1 these differences are ranked according to the time line shown on the abscissa.

Each of these groups of variables imply further consequences. Variance necessitates evaluation of precipitation predictability. This leads to consideration of less certain precipitation in the core of the region compared with more certain water supplies on its northern periphery.

Turning to the human side, the social dissonance of national moods reflects on the reliability of international co-operation which combined with the problems of natural supply determine the availability of each water source. This, in turn, must be matched to the affordability of water and each nation's ability to pay the total bill involved. All such considerations are embedded in the question of the environmental impact each project will have on national economies as well as upon an increasingly fragile planet.

THE REGION DESCRIBED: CORE AND PERIPHERY

A salient feature of the Middle East in Southwest Asia is that it can be sub-divided into the better watered areas of Turkey and Iran, the extremely arid Arabian peninsula, and a zone of transition, the Mashreq, lying in between.[2]

The population of the Mashreq is unevenly distributed in a broad arc including the twin river valleys of the Tigris and Euphrates (Fig. 1-2). This better populated band conforms to the foothills of the Zagros mountains, those of the Anti-Taurus mountains of Turkey, and the highlands of the Levantine shore. The interior of the arc is filled by an extension of the Arabian desert which merges northward into a fluctuating zone of transition, the Syrian steppe. Thus, the area where water uncertainty, population growth, and development converge corresponds to the Fertile Crescent[3] of classical archaeology.

Given such a famous and enticing *nom de terre*, a cautionary note should be sounded. Planners and patriots alike may succumb to ambitious hopes that can at best be only partially fulfilled. Although the western limb of the Fertile Crescent, with its transitional climates and high variance, constitutes the core of this discussion, the area cannot sustain limitless development fuelled by relentlessly increasing populations.

The political units of the Mashreq: Iraq, Israel, Jordan, Lebanon, Palestine (the West Bank and Gaza), and Syria, (alphabetical order) occupy a critical position between Europe, Turkey and North Africa. The environments which they share mark a transition between better watered countries to the north, of which, Turkey is not only contiguous but a major source of international rivers, and the truly arid lands of the Arabian peninsula and north-east Africa to the south. Thus, an important lesson is that the core has elements of both the region to its north and the region to its south and that a mix of water technologies is most appropriate in order to solve its hydrologic problems.

TOPOGRAPHY: CORE AND PERIPHERY [4]

The topography of the Mashreq consists of a central alluvial plain formed by deposits from the Euphrates and Tigris rivers and an open, southward facing arc of mountains and foothills which curve from the Mediterranean sea to the Arabian/Persian Gulf (henceforth referred to as the gulf). The lowland stretches from the headwaters of the Gulf to northern Iraq and into Syria where it is known as the Syrian and Iraqi Jezirah.

A more detailed view beginning in the west reveals a narrow coastal plain which includes the Gaza strip, littoral Israel and the shores of

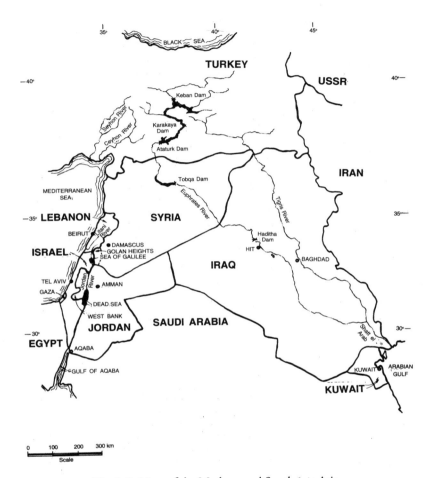

Fig. 1-2: Map o f the Mashreq and Southwest Asia

Lebanon and Syria. This plain is backed in the south by the hills of the West Bank which look eastward over the rift valley of the Dead sea and the Jordan river basin. Beyond the Jordan river rise the hills of the Hashemite kingdom of Jordan which descend gradually to the eastern, central desert.

The hills on both sides of the Jordan valley increase in height to the north with Mount Lebanon to the west in Lebanon and the Golan heights and Mount Hermon to the east. The Jordan river begins in the north with the Hasbani river, a major tributary. (The valley itself is lost to the north in the broken topography of southeast Lebanon.) Farther north and east, the foothills of Syria, marked by the major cities of Damascus, Homs, and Aleppo, give way to the interior lowland. Across a low watershed to the west in Lebanon, the Litani river flows from north to south in the Bekaa valley (a continuation of the rift complex) before turning sharply west to reach the sea. Between the Bekaa and the coastal plain the heights of Lebanon merge northward with the Syrian Jebel Alawi, bordered on the east by the valley of the Asi (Orontes) river and the reclaimed Ghab swamp.

North of coastal Syria, the mountains of Hatay Vilayet (province) in Turkey join the east-west Anti-Taurus range which the Turkish border with Syria and Iraq parallels. These highlands define the northern extent of the Mashreq and provide almost all of the waters of the Euphrates river and nearly half of those of the Tigris. Farther east, the Iran/Iraq border swings south-east following the Zagros mountains from which flow the major tributaries of the Tigris river. These mountains continue along the eastern shore of the gulf, but the Mashreq, itself, is limited by the Arabian desert to the south. Therefore, our tour turns west at the head of the gulf, crossing the desert to end at the hills of Jordan.

HYDROLOGY: CORE TO PERIPHERY

It is within the amphitheatre of the Mashreq as well as in its wings defined by the enclosing mountains that a dramatic search for water is being conducted. The waters originating within the core, as defined above, will not suffice for its future populations and development if current agricultural practices are continued or in a longer view if population growth remains unchecked. As will be shown, they must be augmented by desalination and/or imports from the periphery.

Other means of increasing available supplies, conservation, system repair and maintenance, the recycling of used water, have limited returns. Even water imports will not prevail unless population planning is able to slow the region's swift increase. Nevertheless, each of these elements has its place over time in a comprehensive solution to the problem of supplying water to the people of the core. It thus becomes important to review the hydrology of the entire Mashreq as well as that of its northern periphery.

CLIMATES AND HYDROLOGY

Climates[5]

The climates of the Mashreq are Mediterranean (Csa-Koeppen climate classification), with hot, dry summers and mild, wet winters and 400 to 800 mm of precipitation, and semi-arid steppe (Bsh), having 200 to 400 mm precipitation and cool winters. Both are typified by high variance in precipitation which reflects the changing paths of the jet stream and its attendant rain bearing westerly winds. By the same token, north-south shifts in the sub-tropical high pressure zone, itself responsible for extreme aridity centering upon 30° N latitude, bring periods of drought to the Mashreq. Unpredictable series of arid years are followed by years of bountiful rains. Such was the case when heavy rains and snows in the winter of 1991–2 ended a disastrous multi-year drought. On the other hand, winter rains of such intensity often result in needed water surpluses being lost through flooding which exceeds reservoir capacities.

This climate extends south in a narrow band along the eastern Mediterranean littoral as far as Gaza. It also extends inland to the east, but is greatly modified by higher elevations and a more land-locked situation. To the north in Anatolia a cool and humid, temperate climate (Dsa) with warm summers and cold winters provides 600 to 1000 mm of rain annually with relatively little variance. To the south, the Csa zone merges with the semi-arid steppe (Bsh). Precipitation provides barely enough moisture for dry (fallow) farming on the zone's northern side, and shows increasing variability the farther to the south one travels. Beyond the steppe the arid climate (BWh) of the Arabian desert (with less than 200 mm of rain occurring sporadically, if at all) allows only irrigated agriculture (Fig. 1-3).

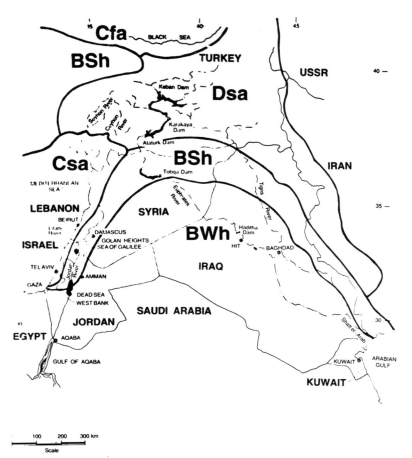

Fig. 1-3: Climates of the Middle East

Variance in precipitation is only one of the challenges that the Mashreq poses. The timing of rainfall and drought is also significant. This is demonstrated by the concept of the water balance which provides a useful overall picture of the problems facing the water managers of the region. Fig. 1-3 shows the water balances for selected stations throughout the Middle East. Note the small potential evapotranspiration (PE) and deficit (i.e., drought) associated with Turkish stations peripheral to the core, the enormous PE and subsequent deficit for stations within the peninsula, and the intermediate values shown for Beirut and other locations within the core. The latter conditions, coupled with variance, where some years may resemble peninsular drought and other years a more northerly situation, emphasize the challenge facing water managers at the core.

Fig. 1-4 shows the diminishing of annual precipitation from north to south on a transect leading from Zonguldak, Turkey, to Aden. A second curve indicates the increasing variance in rainfall as desert conditions are encountered. That is, the drier the climate the more unpredictable precipitation becomes.

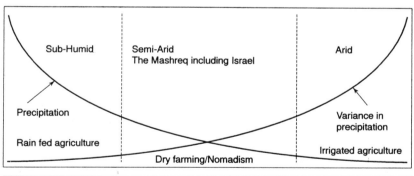

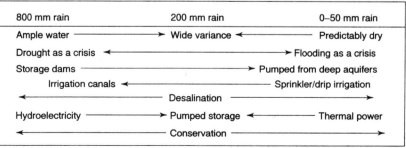

Fig. 1-4: Precipitation and Variability in the Middle East

An initial impression may be that deserts are the least predictable of all environments. A moment's thought, however, reveals that as the predictability of rainfall decreases, the predictability of drought becomes more and more certain. In other words, if one lives in the Sahara or the Arabian peninsula, one should know what to expect, and to prepare for it. But, just as a twenty-five or fifty-year drought wreaks havoc on farmers accustomed to rainfed agriculture, so does the unexpected cloudburst threaten desert inhabitants. The torrential rains and subsequent flooding in parts of upper Egypt in November 1994 are an example of this.[6]

Fig. 1-4 shows that the zone of greatest unpredictability is at the intersection of the precipitation and variance curves. The Anatolian plateau to the north is noted for its rain-fed agriculture and typified by numerous, widely scattered villages. To the south modern sprinkler-fed farms are replacing traditional oases across the Arabian peninsula. Between lies the region which is the focus of this study, the transitional Mashreq with its critical core in which are found truly biblical lands where 'seven years of plenty are followed by seven years of want'.

Hydrology

We must now review the hydrology of the study area in order to appreciate the critical relationship of the core to the periphery.

Precipitation increases from south to north across the entire region both along the Mediterranean shore and in the interior. Kuwait receives an average 111 mm of rain and Baghdad 151 mm. Deir ez-Zor and Hasakah in Syria with 200 mm and 300 mm respectively must rely upon irrigation to insure their crops (Kolars and Mitchell, 1991, Table 9-1). Turkey enjoys an average of 452 mm at Sanliurfa, while Gaziantep (550 mm) and Mardin (686 mm) are within the limits of rain-fed agriculture. Along the Mediterranean littoral Jerusalem averages 492 mm, Beirut 517 mm, Tripoli 745 mm, and Antalya, Turkey 1028 mm. On the Arabian peninsula Aden receives a scant 39 mm, Eilat on the Gulf of Aqaba 27 mm, and Jiddah even less (25 mm). The previous discussion of precipitation variability should be kept in mind, for the aridity of the Arabian peninsula is highly predictable, conditions in the Mashreq are not.

Surface and Underground Waters

Surface water is non-existent in Gaza, and the shallow coastal aquifers have long been over-pumped. The coastal aquifer is said to have had a safe renewable production of 60×10^6 m^3 per year, but current over-pumping is approximately 95×10^6 m^3 annually. This has resulted in seawater intrusion as well as contamination of the aquifer by uncontrolled surface effluents.

Israel fares scarcely better in terms of its water supply within the Green Line, but derives additional waters from the Sea of Galilee and the West Bank (Palestine). Its supplies are so intertwined with those of the West Bank that the situation in the two areas must, therefore, be presented in combination. Sustainable yield of renewable fresh waters in Israel is approximately 1450×10^6 m^3 per annum. Israel had already exceeded this level by the early 1970s, and had to cut 29 per cent from its national water budget (1987×10^6 m^3 in 1987 vs. 1420×10^6 m^3 in 1991) due to severe drought. The sources of its renewable supplies are shown in Tables 1-1, 1-2 and 1-3.

Table 1-1: WATERS USED BY ISRAEL

Source	Availability		Usage
Sea of Galilee			
(Hasbani, Wazani, Dan, side run off)			500×10^6 m^3
West Bank			
Yaqon-Taninim aquifer	340		
Northern aquifer	135		
Nablus-Jenin	70	545	450
Eastern aquifer	125		—
From inside the Green Line			500
(includes the coastal plain aquifer 280)			
Sub-total			1450
Re-cycled			220
Total			1640
West Bank Palestinians			
Surface springs			55×10^6
Wells			25×10^6
Total			80×10^6

Jordan is mining its non-renewable aquifers, removing an estimated 190 mcm in 1990 (Garber and Salameh, 1992, 10–14). The

Disi aquifer in the southeast also is being depleted by heavy pumping on the Saudi side of the border where it is known as the Saq aquifer (Abu Rizaiza, 66–8).

Table 1-2: RENEWABLE WATER SUPPLY ON THE WEST BANK (mcm/yr)

Aquifer	Fresh	Brackish	Total
Eastern	81	70	151
North-east	61	70	131
Mountain	310	40	350
Total	452	180	632

Table 1-3: USE OF WEST BANK WATER (mcm/yr)

Users P/C Share		Fresh	Brackish	Total
Palestinian (West Bank)		90	20	110 + 8*
Israeli	303 (Mtn) 35 (Eastern)			
	Sub-total	338	184 (estimated)	522
Total		428	204	632

Note: Determining the exact amount of available water and the amount of water used on (originating from) the West Bank by both the Palestinians and Israelis is at best a tentative exercise. The above figures are drawn from Baskin (1994) and Assaf et al (1993). A cautionary note is sounded by the latter authors (p. 109), and the wisdom of such a warning is apparent when Baksin's figures are compared internally (as in the above tables). Baskin has done an excellent job of summarizing the water supply and should not be faulted for the differences shown between Table 1-2 and Table 1-3 vis-à-vis fresh and brackish water totals. The differences shown by those totals result from assumptions made by the present authors regarding the estimated amount of brackish water used by Israel.

The Azraq oasis northeast of Amman has also been mined to augment Amman's domestic water supply. Its lake and swamp that were once a stopping place on a major migratory bird flyway were dried up and the groundwater level there dropped seriously. The reversal of the situation in 1994 and the regeneration of the oasis is discussed in Chapter 5, but this happy event is a rare one in Jordan's otherwise bleak picture. Altogether, Jordan's main surface-water supplies from the Yarmouk and other streams amount to about 715 mcm per year with an expected shortfall of 300 mcm by the year 2005 (Kolars, 1992, p. 115).

Lebanon remains reasonably supplied with water. At present an estimated surplus of surface and underground water of over 2,800 mcm exists. However, much of this supply is widely scattered and not easily stored or diverted. A more positive note is that most of its aquifers are quickly renewable given adequate rainfall. Groundwater consumption in 1975—one of the few years for which a record exists—provided 37 per cent of the total amount used. Surface water accounted for 63 per cent (537 mcm). Major rivers have an average flow of 3,700 mcm annually. Of this, 125 mcm reach Israel via the Hasbani. Less appreciated, but nevertheless important, are the waters of the Asi (Orontes) which rise in the Bekaa valley and flow north through Syria and Hatay province, Turkey, to the Mediterranean. Turkey claims that excessive water use in Syria has depleted the Asi to the point where severe water shortages are occuring near Antakya in Hatay province. (*See* Kolars, 1992a).

Syria's situation *vis-à-vis* its water supply remains open to interpretation. Its position between the Jordan basin and better watered Turkey makes it a key geographical link between the core and the periphery. The country is sometimes listed as being rich in water (Falkenmark and Widstrand, 1989), but such comments are based on Syria's large and assured share of the Euphrates river as well as some portion of the Tigris. Its other streams are of relatively little significance.

The Euphrates rises in Turkey where it receives surface flow equaling 88 per cent of the total entering Syria ($29,442 \times 10^9$ m³/yr). Another 12 per cent ($4,015 \times 10^6$ m³/yr) enters the main stream by way of the Balikh, Sajur, and Khabour rivers in Syria. The latter streams, however, receive almost all of their flow from springs whose catchments are in Turkish territory. Therefore, as much as 98 per cent of the Euphrates ($32,788 \times 10^6$ m³/yr) may be subject to upstream withdrawals. The Tigris, of which an estimated 48 per cent (18.3×10^9 m³/yr) originates in Turkey touches Syria for a scant 39 km in the north-east of the country where it forms the border with Turkey and Iraq. As the central of the three riparians on both rivers, Syria has much to gain or lose in the ongoing negotiations regarding the use of these waters, for both Turkey and Iraq have made large claims upon them (Kolars and Mitchell, 1991, Chap. 6).

The show piece of Syrian hydro-development is the Tabqa or Ath-Thawrah Dam on the Euphrates river. Originally intended to supply as much as 60 per cent of Syrian electricity, the dam has been unable to fulfil its promise as the result of low water levels in Lake Assad (its reservoir) resulting from both drought years and upstream activity in Turkey (Cotillon, 1993).

Smaller streams supply the major cities of Syria. The Barada river which serves Damascus has a discharge of 7.4 m³/sec (233 × 10⁶ m³/yr), and consumption of its waters has already passed supply. Aleppo formerly drew water from the Queik river originating in Turkey, but that source has long since been dried up by removals for irrigation in both countries. The city now depends upon water siphoned from Lake Assad as well as additional well water. The Khabour, mentioned above, has a natural flow of 1.8 bcm per year (56.5 m³/sec.), but this amount may be significantly reduced by Turkish withdrawals in the catchment area, or increased by return flow from Turkish fields. Its fate remains to be seen.

Syria has recently built a series of small retaining dams on the headwaters of the Yarmouk river, the downstream portions of which it shares with Jordan, and *de facto* with Israel which diverts between 50 and 125 mcm annually into the Sea of Galilee depending upon the extent of winter flooding. Jordan depends upon water from the Yarmouk for its East Ghor canal which sustains irrigated agriculture along the east bank of the Jordan river. The Johnston Plan awarded Jordan 377 mcm, Syria 90 mcm, and Israel 25 mcm of the Yarmouk (Wolf, 1995, p. 47), though this agreement was never officially recognized and has since begun to fray. In any event, the sharing of the Yarmouk's waters must be resolved along with other water issues facing the nations of the Jordan basin.

Syria also uses significant amounts of groundwater. Springs provide slightly more then 2,000 mcm per year while another 3,500 mcm is pumped from relatively shallow wells. Syrian experts have called for exploration and greater use of deep aquifers, but to date little is known about them (Bakour, 1991, 30–3).

Therefore, Syria, though sometimes listed as water rich, faces uncertainties of supply in the years ahead and is inextricably tied to Turkey by the rivers which the countries share. The latter nation is clearly of vital importance to this study both as a contender for Euphrates waters and as a participant in hydro-diplomacy aimed at supplying water supplements to the core.

Continuing downstream, the twin rivers flow south from Syria through Iraq to their juncture near Qurna in the latter country. Their combined waters form the Shatt al-Arab which flows for another 109 km before entering the gulf east of Bubiyan island. Their volume of 81.9×10^9 m^3 (natural flows: Euphrates = 33,457 mcm; Tigris = 49,200 mcm; Kolars and Mitchell, 1991) rivals that of the Nile at Aswan (84×10^9 m^3).

Like Turkey, Iraq though even further afield, is as intrinsically linked to the problems of water in the Middle East as is Syria. The country is solely dependent upon the combined flows of the Euphrates and Tigris rivers. As indicated above, withdrawals from the Euphrates in Turkey and Syria may significantly reduce the flow of that river into Iraq as well as adding to their pollution. The Tigris river receives 37.6 per cent of its flow directly from Turkey in the main stream. Approximately another 10–12 per cent enters from Turkey via side streams. The remainder enters the left bank from tributaries rising in the Zagros mountains. The waters of the Tigris are reasonably secure from extreme diminution or pollution, but the question of augmenting the flow of the Euphrates remains unresolved, for Iraq feels that it deserves its fair share of the latter river. Syria and Iraq have already agreed that 58 per cent of the Euphrates' flow entering Syria from Turkey will be passed on to Iraq, while 42 per cent can be used in Syria. But the actual volumes involved remain uncertain, in large part due to the high natural variances involved. Just how will the three countries share water in times of severe drought as well as in times of plenty?

A PROLEGOMENON TO HYDRO-POLITICS

Middle Eastern waters fall into three political arenas, those of the Nile basin, those of the Jordan and its tributaries, and those of the Euphrates/Tigris drainages. The waters of a fourth group which originate in Lebanon, the Litani and Orontes (Asi) rivers, are inevitably associated with problems of the Jordan and Euphrates rivers respectively, although each occupies a distinct basin of its own.

We consider the Nile basin, with its ten riparians and the growing demands of Egypt and Sudan, realistically to fall outside the Mashreq and its problems. Numerous people have suggested transferring water from the Nile at least as far as Gaza. However, as of November 1994, personal observation confirmed that even the water destined for Egyptian projects in the Sinai peninsula has yet to cross the Suez canal. Thus, growing domestic needs in Egypt combined with the awakening expectations of sub-Saharan sharers of Nilotic waters places the topic of their use outside our purview.

The sharing of the trans-boundary waters of the Euphrates and Tigris Rivers among Turkey, Syria and Iraq is inherently complex. The Syrians and the Iraqis claim upwards of two-thirds of the Euphrates flow while the Turks seem inclined to offer one-half. The Tigris seems likely to offer surplus water that might resolve this issue, but while the Turks view the two rivers as occupying a single basin, the Arab states insist that the two basins are separate, and at least the Iraqis invoke a policy of no inter-basin transfers. The Turks feel the need to resolve the uses of the Orontes (Asi) which involve use of its headwaters in the Bekaa in Lebanon, the Ghab project in Syria, and shortages in Hatay province in Turkey.

Nevertheless, the waters of Turkey may possibly offer some respite for the nations of the Mashreq. As we propose, there may well be a time when a reasonable and equitable arrangement between Turkey, Syria and Iraq will allow the movement of water southward into the Mashreq. Technically feasible, economically debatable but possible, political decisions must pave the way for such an outcome.

Until then, the focus of the peace process is upon the core of the Middle East as we have defined it. The resolution of its water supply problems is currently paramount, and it is the principles underlying that situation which we will next address.

NOTES

1. We use the term 'Palestine' to refer to the West Bank and Gaza with no predisposition to the eventual outcome of the Middle East peace talks.
2. The region is sometimes called the Arab Mashreq, or in this case it would be the Arab Mashreq plus Israel. In this discussion it will be referred to as the Mashreq. Although Egypt and the Nile are also considered, they present a separate set of conditions and problems which

involve eight other riparian states in Africa (nine others if a small portion of Eritrea is considered: Burundi, Egypt, Eritrea, Kenya, Rwanda, Sudan, Tanzania, Uganda, Zaire). It is unlikely that agreement among all the Nilotic riparians will come easily even for future sharing of Nile waters within the basin itself, let alone agreeing to inter-basin transfers to the northeast.

3. This term is of relatively new origin. James H. Breasted relates, 'There is no name, either geographical or political, which includes all of this great semicircle . . . For historical purposes, some term designating it is indispensable. In his high school history (Ancient Times) therefore the author suggested the term 'Fertile Crescent'. History teachers have found it instructive and convenient and it is now widely used. *The Conquest of Civilization*, Harper & Brothers Publishers (New York and London: MCMXXIV), note p. 117.

4. The discussion which follows is taken from Bakour and Kolars, 1994, 127–35.

5. The waters of the Nile which reach Egypt from the highlands of Ethiopia and the lakes of central Africa are farther removed in space, therefore in time, and furthermore are less accessible in terms of their political milieu. Therefore, discussion of the Nile basin is of limited scope in this study.

6. These rains were local in nature and resulted in heavy *wadi* flooding from the sides of the valley. They did not represent a basin-wide innundation.

2 Water Problems of the Mashreq: A Political Overview

INTRODUCTION

In the practice and theory of international relations co-operation among sovereign states entails risks as well as opportunities. Heads of state and their advisors generally perceive the risks while third parties, promoting co-operation, emphasize the opportunities. More often than not the views of risk-averse political leaders prevail. Co-operation among states is thus a rare occurrence.

Even when it can be demonstrated by some objective measures that co-operation over the long haul will promote the aggregate welfare of the participating parties more than an absence of co-operation, it is still likely that party leaders will reject co-operation because of short-term risks and fears that the other parties will fail to honour their end of the bargain. Co-operative solutions will not be achieved as long as all or most leaders approach negotiations with this mind set. Nevertheless, such negative perceptions on the part of the leaders may be very well-founded.

The possibility of co-operative solutions to the Middle East's growing water crises is subject to the same dynamic. No matter how compelling the 'objective facts', we should not be surprised if co-operation is difficult to achieve. Let us look more closely at the dynamics of co-operation and non-co-operation in the use of international rivers and trans-boundary acquifers.

The benefits of co-operation in river basin development are typically highly asymmetrical. For example, Egypt receives all its water from the Nile river but Zaire's share of the Nile basin is of negligible importance to its overall water balance. Such combinations of asymmetry and multiple bargaining parties (for example, ten sovereign nations, now including Eritrea, share the Nile basin) render voluntary co-operative solutions extremely difficult. When water is the sole focus of negotiations, gains and losses become apparent in a very real sense. The recognition of such consequences can lead to paralysis and the non-resolution of the collective action dilemma.[1]

However, when progress is achieved, asymmetries in benefits can be so great that one riparian may agree to bear all or most of the cost of a co-operative solution. Such was the case when Egypt financed the construction of the Jebel Aulia storage dam on the White Nile, just upstream of Khartoum in 1932, and of the raising of the Owen Falls dam in Uganda in the early 1950s. Much more recently, on 3 September 1987, Jordan and Syria signed an agreement for the construction of the Wehda dam on the Yarmouk, under which Jordan accepted the full cost of construction and the payment of compensation to those displaced by the project in Syria, and also agreed to give Syria 75 per cent of all power generated at the dam site. This accord has not been implemented, as Israel is not a party to it, and has been superseded by the peace treaty between Jordan and Israel, signed 26 October 1994.

Asymmetries exist across time as well as in relative degrees of dependence on the resource. Supply or quality crises may drive some riparians to seek co-operation as a matter of the highest urgency, while other riparians can afford to wait. Those most pressed must manipulate incentives and disincentives to bring the less-pressed to the bargaining table. In the countries of the core and periphery with which we are concerned the relative degrees of urgency defining the search for a co-operative solution can be displayed in the following manner:

Relative Urgency for a Co-operative Solution

Gaza-Jordan-West Bank-Israel-(Egypt)-Syria-Iraq-Turkey- Lebanon

Present- -Future

Degrees of urgency are determined by differing combinations of variables. For Gaza, existing supplies from aquifers are being used at unsustainable rates while quality is declining rapidly. A remedy needs to be found now. By contrast, Lebanon's major sources of water come from rainfall and the Litani river which lies entirely within its borders. It has no need to import water nor to deal with other riparians, although shortages in the Shi'ite south remain a source of unrest, and as such may serve as an internationally significant destabilizing influence. Jordan is already dealing with a supply and quality crisis. The

West Bank must establish legal claims to some part of its water resources which, depending on Israeli and Jordanian counter-claims, may or may not be adequate to meet anticipated needs. Israel must assure its future supply, and this can be done either through transfers from neighbours or through desalination. Most of Syria's present water use comes from rainfall and small rivers and *wadis*, but much of its projected water demand will depend on the Euphrates and Tigris, both of which require agreements with Turkey. Egypt has a legally guaranteed supply of 55.5 billion m³, but it has projected additional needs that could be met either through more efficient use of its current supply or increased supply from its upstream neighbours. Year to year variance in the flow of the Nile can still be a problem, as the drought of the 1980s and the 1994 floods demonstrate, although the latter were driven by local rains rather than basin-wide innundation. Iraq is blessed with large amounts of surface waters, but its delivery infrastructure is concentrated on the Euphrates. It would rather have its acquired rights in that river recognized by Turkey than invest in water transfers from the Tigris to the Euphrates. Turkey likewise has abundant surface waters but with one of the largest populations in the region (*ca.* 61 million) and rapidly growing urban centres, it already faces a growing energy shortage the solution to which is associated in part with increased hydro-electric production.

One way out of such asymmetries is through multi-good bargaining. The bargaining agenda is made more complicated so that disparities in the benefits of co-operation with respect to one good can be overcome or at least obscured by deals struck with respect to other goods. These exchanges may be quite straightforward, such as Iraqi oil for 'Turkish' water. Less obvious would be Palestinian recognition of Israel in partial exchange for recognized rights to West Bank water; Syrian control of Kurdish insurgent raids into Turkey in partial exchange for Euphrates water; Israeli technical know-how in water conservation for a part of the water saved (Kally and Tal, 1989); Egyptian good offices in raising external assistance for all states in the Nile basin in exchange for a binding agreement regarding Egypt's water claims.[2]

But what of involuntary solutions? Co-operation can be imposed. International relations theory refers to these as hegemonic solutions. A pattern of resource use is elaborated by the dominant power in the basin and imposed on the others. Colonial powers have been such hegemonies, defining rights and obligations across the jurisdictional boundaries of their empires. The British devised an imposed regime for all of the Nile basin (although Ethiopia was never fully integrated into it) as did the Soviet Union in the basins of the Amu Darya and Syr Darya. In the region that concerns us here, it can be argued that Israel has imposed a solution in the Jordan basin, that Turkey may be in a position to do so in the Euphrates basin (and to a lesser extent in that of the Tigris), and that Egypt has acted as a quasi-hegemon in the Nile basin.

It will be noted that the three examples cited include an upstream state (Turkey), a mid-stream state (pre-1967 Israel) and a downstream state (Egypt). Although geographical asymmetries are powerful, position in the basin does not therefore fully determine bargaining power. Unsurprisingly, other resources come into play (Naff and Matson, 1984 and Frey, 1992). If position, military power, and economic resources are all joined in one state, its writ will run in the basin. On the other hand, military and economic power may be so concentrated in states in less favourable locations in the basin that they can impose their own solution (Israel) or so that more favourably located states will think twice before tampering with a strong downstream state's 'rights' (Ethiopia in relation to Egypt).

Somewhere between voluntary and involuntary solutions, and potentially associated with both, are induced solutions. This brings a third party into the bargaining process. It may be a superpower interested not so much in the resource issue *per se* but rather in solving it to further some other purpose. In 1972 the Soviet Union sought to reconcile Syria and Iraq, both countries in which the USSR had a large political and military stake, concerning joint use of the Euphrates. In this instance an induced settlement was not achieved. Similarly today, the US continues to promote multilateral talks on water issues among the actors in the Arab-Israeli theatre on the assumption that progress toward a co-operative solution in this domain may create an atmosphere conducive to an overall settlement.

To date the most effective agents of induced co-operation have been multilateral funding institutions, particularly the World Bank. The Bank has tried, to the extent possible, to condition its financing of large hydraulic projects in international river basins on the prior negotiation of co-operative agreements among the riparian states. This policy was successful in the case of the Nile in 1959 but so far has been unsuccessful with respect to Turkey's Southeast Anatolia

Project (Turkish acronym: GAP), where development has gone ahead without an accord and without Bank funding. In the case of the Yarmouk, the World Bank (and the United States Agency for International Development) continue to attempt to induce an accord among Syria, Jordan and Israel.

Co-operative solutions, whether arrived at voluntarily, induced or imposed, are very difficult to achieve, and once achieved, difficult to maintain. Only in the Nile basin have any significant successes been registered.[3] But the recent literature that predicts acute conflict in the absence of co-operation (Starr, Bullock and Darwish, Hamid Sa'id al-Maw'ad) fails to specify the real dangers. It tends to invoke what may be called the Fashoda syndrome, harking back to the famous incident in 1898 in which General Kitchener met Colonel Marchand on the brink of what seemed to be a possible colonial war for control of the headwaters of the Nile. The problem is that it is not at all easy for one riparian in a drainage basin to deprive another of significant amounts of water, and it is not at all easy to define the military goals to be pursued if there is a resort to force. Again, the nature of trans-boundary rivers creates special characteristics of military encounters that they may engender (Biswas, 1982; Gurr, 1985).

First, to deprive another state of the use of an international river, a riparian must be able to cut off or divert the flow of the river. This costs money and may be as disruptive to portions of the population of the state undertaking the action as it is to the inhabitants of the targeted state. Second, the storage facility or diversionary works may be vulnerable to air, artillery or ground attack, although the Geneva conventions and other principles of the conduct of war expressly forbid targeting such works. The authors have not found cases in which they consider the works themselves to be the *casus belli* (ILC, 1991). Finally, water cannot be stored indefinitely without endangering the storage facilities themselves through excessive accumulations of subsequent high water, or conversely the supply's being depleted through seepage and/or evaporation.

For the most part, water disputes in the Middle East have remained below the military level with two exceptions. The first was the Fashoda incident, which was resolved without bloodshed. The second was Israel's attack over the period 1964 to 1966 on the works in Syria that were being undertaken to divert the headwaters of the Jordan. That project was abandoned. However, there have been a number of tense moments. In 1925, after the assassination of the Sirdar, Lee Stack, by Egyptian nationalists, Britain punished Egypt by allowing Sudan to begin to design the Sennar dam on the Blue Nile and the irrigation grid that was to become the Gezira scheme (Waterbury, 1979, p. 65). The next bellicose incident, aside from the Israeli attacks of 1964–6, came in 1975 when Iraq mobilized for war as Syria began to fill the reservoir upstream of the Thawra (Tabqa) dam.[4] The Arab League intervened to mediate the dispute. After the Camp David accords, there was talk of Nile waters being delivered to Israel's Negev. This elicited a hostile declaration on the part of the Ethiopian government, to which President Sadat responded with a warning that any state that tampered with Egypt's water supply would risk a military response (cited in Rogers, 1991, p. 22). Finally, when Iraq occupied Kuwait in 1990, it is claimed that Lord Owen urged Turkey to restrict the flow of the Euphrates to Iraq. If such advice was given, Turkey did not heed it.

No matter how acute the crises that may emerge in the coming years over water supply in the Middle East, armed conflict is not likely to be an outcome. Unilateral diversions of the Euphrates have taken place in both Syria and Turkey without an effective military response from Iraq. Whatever arrangements emerge from the current negotiations over water in the Jordan basin, no riparian is likely to be able to challenge Israeli hegemony in the foreseeable future, although mitigating circumstances appear to make such a perceived need unnecessary. Only in the Nile basin, where Ethiopia, perhaps a decade or more from now, might divert significant amounts of Blue Nile water for purposes of irrigation, could we see tensions mount.

In the absence of co-operative arrangements, it is likely that various riparians will pursue costly unilateral solutions to their supply problems that will be indisputably sub-optimal in economic terms. Resources will be misallocated within riparian states and across the basins as a whole. New supply-demand equilibria will not be achieved through warfare and seizure of water resources but rather through disruptive adjustments within riparian states. Agricultural production will be re-configured or curtailed, aquifers will be mined, and costly treatment plants installed to salvage or re-utilize a relatively fixed supply of water of deteriorating quality. Still another solution, a more rational regional division of agricultural production, will not be explored.

RE-CONFIGURING AGRICULTURE

The same risk-aversion that characterizes the difficulties in achieving co-operation in the use of international waters also is a hallmark of agricultural policy in the Middle East. Relying on international markets for substantial supplies of food introduces an element of vulnerability that few regional states are willing to accept. Because they have no feasible choice, Israel and Jordan are already far down the path of trading internationally for food. Other countries have rejected economic arguments of comparative advantage and have subsidized the cultivation of many agricultural commodities. These all have a high cost in terms of water. The present demand for water in the Middle East is not primarily driven by growing populations, nor by increasing standards of living, but rather by the so-far unsuccessful efforts undertaken to feed these populations from local production. As Peter Beaumont graphically puts it, if 183 irrigated hectares in Egypt were taken out of production, enough water would be freed up to provide drinking water to a million people for a year (Beaumont, 1994).

The argument here is by no means to put an end to agriculture but to re-configure it. To do so requires that water be assigned a value in the calculation of production costs and rates of return. Both Israel and Jordan have taken modest steps in this direction, but Syria and Egypt have not, and the West Bank and Gaza have not yet been given the chance. Egypt supplies to water its farmers without charge. The real cost of delivery may be $0.03–0.05/m^3$. A hectare of irrigated wheat using $12,000$ m^3, would bear water costs of $360–600$, and yield on average four tons of grain. Those four tons could be bought on the international market for $750 in 1993 prices (Beaumont, 1994). Syria not only subsidizes water but pays wheat farmers a premium over international prices: in recent years between $360 and $661 per ton as contrasted with *ca.* $200 on international markets (Khaldi, 1992). Peter Hazell et al. (1994) have estimated elasticities of demand for agricultural water in Egypt, and show that if a doubling of price from 5 piastres to 10 piastres per m^3 were made (i.e., from 2 to 4¢) demand for water would decrease by 8 bcm. 'The model utilized in this study shows that if farmers were to pay the full economic price for their water, total water use in agriculture would drop sharply, yet at little cost to agricultural income' (Hazell et al, 1994, p. 19).

Considering water a factor of production like land, labour, capital, and technology would enhance efficiency in its use and force a search for those agricultural products that yield the highest return. It is equally true that such a consideration would lead to the abandonment of some kinds of agriculture that are water-intensive and of low market value. It would limit land reclamation projects to those that reliably produce high-value crops proximate to their markets.

There are several factors that militate against such a re-configuration. We have already noted that the principle of acquired rights in the use of international water courses provides no incentive to conserve water nor to use it more efficiently. Second, the agrarian sectors of the societies under consideration have all nurtured vested interests over time. The most powerful politically may be the most recent in terms of their control of agricultural assets. Private commercial farmers in Egypt's reclaimed areas, coupled with the four million or so farm families in the old lands, while not themselves allied, must be taken into account in any calculus of the political costs of re-configuration. Similarly, several highly placed Jordanians have important stakes in the East Ghor project that would make unlikely any attempt to pass on the operating costs of the canal to the beneficiaries. Although its symbolic importance appears to be receding, the *kibbutz* movement in Israel, so central to the notion of constructing the new Zionist society, still exercises some claims to special treatment in terms of subsidies. Finally, Syria's Ba'ath party regime is often depicted as relying on a small holder, peasant base, which in turn may explain the political attractiveness of subsidizing small holder farming through free water and high farm gate purchase prices.

None of these constraints, even in combination, is insurmountable. Agrarian lobbies are neither well organized nor more significant politically than urban populations. The argument that Islam forbids the appropriation and sale of water is not convincing in that the right to use water can be, and is, appropriated and water sold throughout the Middle East. Egyptians may be much less familiar with water sales than Jordanians or Palestinians, but it is doubtful that exacting some sort of charge for water delivery would provoke a religiously-inspired backlash.

THE ROLE OF LAW

For co-operation's sake, it is fortunate that few states can adopt consistent legal stances because their geographic positions are themselves varied. For example, Syria is mid-stream on the Euphrates and the Orontes but upstream on the Jordan. The Yarmouk forms part of its boundary with Jordan. Syria may sympathize with Palestinian claims to full control of the surface waters of the West Bank, the bulk of which currently drain into the Israeli coastal aquifer, but Syria itself is the beneficiary of a cross-frontier aquifer (the Ras al-'Ain) which drains from Turkey into northern Syria. Similarly, Turkey controls the headwaters of the Euphrates and the Tigris but is the downstream state in the Orontes (a relatively minor consideration for Turkey given the Orontes' small annual discharge of some 570 mcm).[5] Israel, although it has captured the headwaters of the Jordan (but not of the Yarmouk), is faced with the possibility of giving up that control one day, and therefore cannot take a firm stand for sovereign upstream rights. Moreover, if that principle is extended to the aquifer that drains the West Bank, a future Palestinian state might challenge Israel's acquired rights.

In the Middle East and elsewhere, international law comes into play mainly to sustain bargaining positions already adopted by contending parties. On the one hand, we have the discredited but still invoked Harmon Doctrine laid down by the US Attorney General Judson Harmon in 1895. He opined that there were no principles of international law that would oblige the US to take into consideration Mexico's needs with respect to the Rio Grande. He continued that any concessions the US might make to those needs would be based on 'comity' rather than international law and thus would not constitute a legal precedent. On the other hand the concept of the community of basin interests, with an attendant right of any riparian to block unilateral actions by any other, is straight-forward but so fraught with the prospect of paralysis that few nations have endorsed it.

The middle ground, where most states feel most comfortable, is governed by principles that are the difficult to define in operational terms. This ground is defined by the concept of limited territorial sovereignty, itself rooted in the classical injunction *sic utere tuo ut alienum non laedas*: 'thus use what is yours so as not to cause harm to another'. A corollary is that a riparian should make a good faith effort to obtain the acquiescence of other riparians in the basin to water projects it wishes to undertake, but that these riparians enjoy no legal right of veto. The Lake Lanoux arbitration of 1957 between France and Spain invoked 'the rules of good faith' that enjoin any riparian to take into consideration the interests of other riparians to the extent compatible with the pursuit of its own interests (Michael, 1974, p. 53). In turn the guiding principles of 'good faith' are avoidance of causing appreciable harm to other riparians and the pursuit of equitable or reasonable use.

Herein lies the problem. There are no broadly accepted definitions of what is appreciably harmful, nor equitable and reasonable. In the most important attempt to operationalize these concepts, the Helsinki Rules of 1966 [*see* International Law Association (ILA, 1967), and International Law Commission (ILC, 1979)] lay out eleven principles to guide water use. These range from the social and economic needs of populations, to established patterns of use, to geography. No single principle takes priority over another.

Let us look at some specific Middle Eastern examples. Turkey invokes equity in developing irrigation in the backward region of southeast Anatolia while Iraq invokes appreciable harm to established patterns of use and the need to protect its committed infrastructural and social costs. Who is to choose between the equity aspects of absorbing Soviet Jews into the Israeli economy and the harm that their demand for water may cause Palestinians? Is it 'reasonable' for Egypt to cultivate sugar-cane when Sudan can cultivate it with much less surface water? How does one choose between long-term economic returns and short-term social welfare concerns, or between the welfare of future generations and that of the present?

One may extract or infer from various official reports and newspaper accounts the following principles or interests advanced by Middle Eastern riparians to defend or lay claim to shares of trans-boundary waters:

a. economic potential, future acreage: Ethiopia, Sudan, Syria, Turkey
b. existing acreage: Egypt, Iraq, Israel
c. existing population: Egypt
d. per capita water availability: Syria, Turkey
e. equity, national security: Egypt, Israel, Lebanon, Turkey[6]
f. Harmon Doctrine: Ethiopia, Israel, Turkey

In the 1991 report of the ILC, the section on the law of the non-navigational uses of 'international water courses' revisited and extended the Helsinki rules (*see* ILC, 1991, 152–98). However, the report does not break new ground. It condenses but does not modify the eleven guidelines of the ILA Helsinki Rules; it cites the obligation not to cause appreciable harm and the obligation to co-operate, largely if not exclusively through the exchange of data. It sets forth rules of notification of unilateral initiatives, providing a six-month waiting period for replies and protests, and another six-month period of obligatory negotiations. Significantly the report makes no provision for failed negotiations; presumably in the event of failure the initiator is free to proceed, having made a good faith effort to obtain approval.

There have been a few attempts to operationalize various criteria of equitable use and appreciable harm. The most parsimonious is Peter Rogers' in which he applies Baumol's measure of 'super fairness'[7] to international water resources (Rogers, 1991). He successfully determines a 'core'[8] that is dependent on measuring only economic returns to the riparians involved. It does not directly address or quantify issues of security and non-material preferences.

A more elaborate set of measures has been advanced by James Moore (1992) utilizing four variables — population, existing patterns of water utilization (i.e., acquired rights), natural flow, and shares in recharge area. As he notes, there is no standard by which one can weigh the relative importance of these four variables in determining an equitable allocation of the resource, but by weighing them equally he is able to minimize the 'error distance' of a range of solutions from a 50–50 division of the resource.

Finally, Nurit Kliot (1994) tackles the Helsinki Rules' guideline head on, attributing numerical scores to thirteen variables directly or indirectly derived from them. However, like Moore's operationalization, Kliot does not assign weights to the variables and, as suggested above, it is precisely because riparian nations will differ on the relative importance of variables that the Helsinki rules will break down as effective guidelines to co-operative solutions.

There is one distributional principle that has some currency in practice, mainly because it can be measured in both quantitative and qualitative terms. It is that of acquired rights, i.e., prior usage, or the conferral of quasi-property rights to water on the basis of demonstrated use over time.[9] This principle can only be challenged by invoking an allegedly superior need that we will term economic potential.

Whereas acquired rights, both to the waters of rivers and aquifers, are most often invoked by downstream states which first exploited the waters, upstream states, whose claims to water come historically much later, are apt to invoke economic potential. In the periphery of the region with which we are concerned, there are two dyads of states locked in dispute over these principles: Egypt and the Sudan in the Nile basin, and Iraq and Turkey on the Euphrates. The acquired rights of Egypt and Iraq, the downstream states, are based on millennia of demonstrated use. By contrast, the Sudan and Turkey argue that the vast economic potential of their underdeveloped, irrigable regions, between the Blue and White Nile for Sudan, and in southeast Anatolia, generate legitimate claims to water that should supersede or counterbalance acquired rights. Turkey also has resorted to claims of unrestricted territorial sovereignty as embodied in the Harmon Doctrine.

The contrast, however, is not as sharp as indicated above because even the upstream states implicitly acknowledge the power of claims derived from acquired rights, as does Israel which can now cite thirty years of use of the upper Jordan (albeit contested) through the national water carrier and perhaps twenty-five years based on annual abstractions from the Yarmouk, as well as long-term use of the waters of the Yargon Taninim aquifer which descends from the West Bank to the Israeli coastal plain.

The point is that the principle of acquired rights gives any riparian an incentive to increase use and to establish new, water-intensive projects in order to come to the bargaining table with as strong a position as possible. Recall that Sudan's acquired rights, first codified in 1929, were based on the unilateral development of the Gezira over the protests of the Egyptian government.

Similarly, the acquired rights principle provides little incentive to conserve water and to use it more efficiently. If one is able to do more with the same or less amount of water, then the logic of acquired rights is undermined because their normative underpinning is the idea that any reduction in the acquired amounts will have significant welfare costs. Doing more with less suggests that the absolute amounts at stake may not bear directly on welfare, thereby posing the open-ended question as to just what amount is necessary for the population's welfare.

The disincentives to efficiency are particularly important when one approaches the issue of re-configuring the use of water in agriculture (discussed earlier). However, in the core area increased demand and constraints on supply have created such severe imbalances that the need to conserve has overwhelmed the logic of establishing new use rights through new water-intensive projects. It is, rather, in the periphery that this logic may still prevail.

It is rightly part of folk wisdom that threesomes are particularly unstable groups whether among children, consenting adults, or nations. In the Euphrates, the Jordan, and the Nile basins, the game is played primarily among triads: Turkey, Syria, and Iraq; Jordan, Syria, and Israel; Egypt, Sudan, and Ethiopia. There are disincentives to co-operation among triads, because virtually any combination of two against one can provide a dominant coalition that can impose its solution upon the third. Any member of the triad has an incentive not to commit to co-operation in order to extract the highest possible price for it and will threaten to ally with the other member of the triad if it is denied its price. Once it has committed itself it loses its bargaining leverage unless it threatens to defect. Thus the tendency is for no member of the triad to commit to any other. Only when one of them is as powerful or more powerful than the other two combined can a hegemonic solution be imposed. Turkey approaches that position on the Euphrates, while Israel is hegemonic on the Jordan though only in the purely military sense. Egypt cannot impose its will upon both Sudan and Ethiopia and probably upon neither. Egypt's nightmare is that Sudan and Ethiopia ally in the use of the Blue Nile. Sudan, however, would probably rather bargain with both Egypt and Ethiopia without committing itself to either. One will immediately recognize that Sudan thereby penalizes itself doubly: it denies itself the benefits of tripartite co-operation as well as those of selling its co-operation to one partner.

In sum, no matter how compelling the logic of co-operation, it is most likely to come about through imposition or inducement, not through enlightened voluntary action. Material inducements from outside the arena of conflict can alter the asymmetries that characterize relations among the contending parties. But there is another facet of inducement to which this report directly speaks. We may know the objective facts of a conflict situation: who controls what armed force and of what quality; the geo-strategic givens of the situation; the relative technological capacities of the contending forces, etc. These constitute a measurable *rapport de forces*. However, how leaders perceive this reality is as important as objective reality. Both history and recent experience may shape how leaders define degrees of vulnerability or of capability. Grievances of the past may be taken as grievances of the present. But crucial variables such as available technology, the changing weights of productive sectors in the economy, fertility, and population growth rates may have changed fundamentally the context in which co-operation is sought.

This means that advocates of alternative dispute resolution are, in the final analysis, concerned with changing the perceptions of the negotiating parties to better reflect new realities and new possibilities. Second track diplomacy cannot change the *rapport de forces*, but it can change how leaders and citizenries perceive what is achievable within a given balance of power (Delli Priscoli, 1992, p. 11). There is no magic here. Co-operation in these terms will not mean that all parties are equal but rather that all parties may improve their well being.

NEEDS-BASED CRITERIA FOR EQUITABLE WATER SHARING SETTLEMENTS

Many of the common initial claims for water rights are based either on geography, i.e., from where a river or aquifer originates and how much of that territory falls within a certain state, or on chronology, i.e. who has been using the water the longest. The extreme positions of either definition have been referred to as 'the doctrine of absolute sovereignty' in the first case, stating that a state has absolute rights to water flowing through its territory, and 'prior appropriation' in the second, that is 'first in time, first in right'.[10]

These conflicting doctrines of geography and chronology clash along all of the international rivers surveyed, with positions usually defined by relative riparian positions. Downstream riparians, such as Iraq and Egypt, often receive less rainfall than their upstream neighbours and therefore have depended on river-water for much longer historically. As a consequence, modern 'rights based' disputes often take the form of upstream riparians such as Ethiopia and Turkey arguing in favour of the doctrine of absolute sovereignty, with downstream riparians taking the position of prior appropriation.

In many water disputes which have been resolved, however, the paradigms used for negotiations have not been 'rights based'. In agreements between Egypt and Sudan signed in 1929 and 1959, for example, allocations were arrived at on the basis of local needs, primarily of agriculture. Egypt argued for a greater share of the Nile because of its larger population and extensive irrigation works. Current allocations reflect these needs.

Likewise along the Jordan river, the Johnston accord, although not ratified, emphasized the needs rather than the inherent rights of each of the riparians. Johnston's approach, based on a report performed under the direction of the Tennessee Valley Authority, was to estimate, without regard to political boundaries, the water needs for all irrigable land within the Jordan valley basin which could be irrigated by gravity flow. National allocations were then based on these in-basin agricultural needs, with the understanding that each country could then use the water as it wished, including to divert it out of basin. This was not only an acceptable formula to the parties at the time, but it allowed for a break-through in negotiations when a land survey of Jordan concluded that its future water needs were lower than previously thought.

One pattern which emerges, is that most international water negotiations begin with differing legal interpretations of geography and chronology, and yet, all of the settlement of negotiations regarding the rivers as shown in Table 2-1, with the exception of the Mekong, rely to some extent on a needs based measure for criteria for water allocations. These latter observations suggest potentially useful strategies at the negotiating table.

Table 2-1: CRITERIA FOR WATER ALLOCATIONS

Basin	Criteria
Ganges	Percentage of flow during dry season
Indus	Historic and planned use (for Pakistan) plus geographic allocations
Jordan (Johnston Plan)	Amount of irrigable land within the watershed; countries could then use water how and where they wished, including out of basin
Mekong	Allocations have not been an issue; 'reasonable and equitable use' for the basin defined in detail since 1975
Nile	Acquired rights plus even division of any additional water resulting from development projects

NOTES

1. While excluded from the overall discussion, Egypt and the Nile river are included at this point for purposes of comparative analysis.

2. We list these as examples stated by others, and make no claims as to their alleged authority.

3. Even hegemons are seldom the unitary actors the term implies. Robert Collins (1990) shows how divided British colonial officialdom was in the early 20th century with respect to the Nile. Officials in Uganda, Sudan and Egypt often came to promote 'their country's' interests. The hegemonic solution thus tended to be the result of bargaining among colonial dependencies rather than a blueprint produced in London.

4. The Syrian action coincided with Turkish filling of the Keban reservoir and a year of heavy drought. Both events exacerbated the Syrian/Iraqi situation.

5. The figure given represents flow altered by human activity. Natural flow of the Orontes in Turkish Hatay might be as high as 1,100 mcm/yr but for upstream removals. *See* Kolars, 'Water Resources of the Middle East', p.112. Turkish reports indicate that present flow into Turkey may be far less than the amount given in this discussion.

6. This rubric is not self-evident for Turkey and Lebanon. For the first, the GAP project is both an equity and a security issue in that all the 'neglected' populations of south-east Anatolia are to benefit, but especially the Kurdish populations, parts of which currently constitute a threat to Turkey's internal security. Likewise Lebanon needs to use the Litani to develop the Shi'ite south of the country upon which the future stability of the 'third' Lebanese republic will depend (Kubursi and Amery, 1992).

7. Super fairness obtains when no party to a co-operative solution would prefer to trade its benefits for those of another party. In Roger's application, returns to the use of water, i.e., a single-good bargain, determine the net benefits. It might complicate formalization, but simplify reaching a solution, if the core (in game theoretic terms) were determined in a multi-good bargain.

8. The term 'core' in this case is drawn from economic theory and refers to that area where the preference curves of two or more parties overlap. Within this 'core' no party would want to trade its benefits for those of any of the other parties. This usage should not be confused with the core of periphery and core used throughout this study.

9. Daniel Hillel summarizes the several terms alluding to water rights as follows:

    (1) absolute sovereignty—each state has an unrestrained right to use the water resources within its own territory, (2) riparian rights—every

state along the course of a river has an inherent right to the water of that river, which is not to be diminished or degraded without that state's concurrence, (3) river integrity—all riparians are required to preserve the natural course of the river and utilize it within the natural watershed rather than divert waters out of the basin, (4) historical rights—(i.e., prior rights, authors) a state that had used the resource consistently in the past has the right to continue using it; (5) optimal development (i.e., economic potential, authors)—each river basin should be developed optimally as an integrated hydrological unit (Hillel, 1994, 270).

10. The comments in this section are drawn from Wolf, 1995.

3 Economics, Population and the Environment

Political considerations may seem to be the overwhelming issue in any discussion of Middle Eastern water. However, in the final analysis, economic constraints and possibilities, population growth and changes in levels of living (with accompanying changes in water consumption), and the impact of demand, supply and disposal upon the fragile environments of the region will ultimately determine, far more than politics, the uses of regional water supplies. It is with this in mind that the following comments are presented.

POPULATION: THE EXPLOSION THAT IS NOT

The reader may be momentarily reassured by the title of this section, or may be appalled by the authors' seeming naïveté. We intend neither interpretation. Our point is that the popular phrase, 'the population explosion' is dangerously misleading. An explosion releases its energy in one catastrophic instant. Its survivors pick themselves up and set about restoring order and going on with their lives. Population growth is just the opposite. Its progress is slow at first and its impact difficult to detect. Only as time passes does the devastation resulting from it occur. By that time, little can be done, for even low rates of increase in population which would seem desirable at the beginning result in large increments if the base upon which they are computed is enormous. In this case, the base upon which they are computed far exceeds the carrying capacity of the environment upon which the given population depends.

An analogy between population growth and the famous 'Man in the Iron Mask' would be more accurate. His head was locked in a metal mask as a form of punishment. Though uncomfortable, the situation was at first bearable, but with the passage of time, his beard and hair grew and grew and gradually began to suffocate him. A tiny increment of growth each day eventually became an overwhelming problem. So too with population in the Mashreq. When all else is said and done, when all the water projects are in place and all the available water delivered and recycled and conserved, when agriculture has completely given way to domestic use, a critical shortage of water for human consumption will persist unless population growth stabilizes.

The relationship between population and water availability in the Mashreq is a direct one. There are three basic uses for fresh (i.e., sweet) water: human consumption and necessary domestic use (i.e., bathing and cleaning[1]), agriculture, and industrial uses. At present, agriculture (i.e., irrigation) accounts for 70 to 90 per cent of all the water consumed in the region. This in turn relates to the perceived need for food security based on irrigated agriculture. It may be argued that with the exception of Turkey (on the periphery) none of the nations in question is self sufficient in food. Even today, every country must import food, and its supply and security is already a matter of continuing activity and negotiation. Despite all manner of problems, the food keeps coming. A total food embargo would be almost impossible to enforce or maintain in today's world. Therefore, we consider the question of food security as moot, and by extension, agree that for the near future there should be sufficient water for domestic and industrial purposes through conservation, recycling, and reasonable decreases in agriculture.[2]

This idea may be further amplified through consideration of conservation. For example, during recent drought years Israel reduced its use of agricultural water by 39 per cent without parallel losses in net agricultural output (Chapter 5). By the same token, it is unlikely that any of the Mashreq countries will develop industries that will become major consumers of water. Pollution from small industrial sources may still pose a problem, but, given the critical nature of the situation, should be quickly controlled.

Nevertheless, while conservation and improved technology (water applications and new drought resistant species) are necessary components of any action plan, in the long term such measures will not suffice. The poor distribution of water resulting from geographical location and/or political inequities still must be resolved. Beyond such solutions, unchecked population growth remains the ultimate threat to water sufficiency. This discussion attempts to lay out in terms of absolute population growth the dimensions of water consumption, real and pending, for the countries of the Mashreq.

The sobering impact of population growth is made evident in Table 3-1. High and low growth estimates based on 1991 data have been used to compute future populations for Israel, Jordan, the West Bank, and Gaza. Water consumption is then equated with estimated populations. Low water demand shown in the table assumes that urban use grows at current per capita usage; high demand allows 100 cubic metres per capita per year for urban use. The low rate of population growth assumes that one million Israeli immigrants reached Israel by 1993; the high rate assumes that two million immigrants will arrive by the year 2000. Jordan is assumed to have received 300,000 refugees shortly after the Gulf war, the West Bank's low rate of growth assumes no immigration; the high rate assumes 600,000 immigrants between 1995 and 2005. Gaza is assumed to receive no immigration.

Projections of individual nation's growth rates are presented in the table. The critical insight to be gained is what to expect if high rates of growth occur. By the year 2020 Israel can expect an absolute water deficit—that is current annual natural potential minus projected demand—of 800 mcm. The Israelis anticipate meeting this demand through improved technology and intensive sea water desalination. On the other hand, they assert that they cannot relinquish any of the major water sources upon which Israel now depends.

Jordan's deficit could reach 730 mcm in the same period of time. This deficit alone would be double its present total consumption. Desalination cannot serve all the country's needs, for its only contact with the sea is at Aqaba. While the water projects suggested in the second part of this book could satisfy local demands for that port, the cost of pumping water from either Dead Sea desalination plants or from those proposed for Aqaba to Amman and other northern cities would be prohibitive. Thus, the importation of water from the periphery, as suggested in Chapter 7, becomes plausible.

The hydrologic future of Palestine (the West Bank and Gaza) is even less certain. There will be an absolute deficit of 395 mcm without immigration and 525 mcm if the suggested immigration were to take place. Gaza alone will need an additional 60 to 180 mcm by the year 2020, and this assumes that the natural supplies of water there will

Table 3-1: PROJECTED POPULATION AND WATER DEMAND[11]

Entity	Population (millions)	Water Needs Low Demand[a] (mcm/yr)	Water Needs High Demand[a] (mcm/yr)	Low/High Water Deficit[b] (mcm/yr)
		Israel		
1 million immigrants:[c]				
1991	4.80	1800	1800	200/200
2000	6.44	2000	2000	400/400
2020	8.85	2200	2200	600/600
2 million immigrants:[c]				
1991	4.80	1800	1800	200/200
2000	7.46	2100	2100	500/500
2020	10.01	2400	2400	800/800
		Jordan		
300,000 refugees				
1991	3.60	870	980	0/110
2000	4.91	960	1100	90/230
2020	9.76	1300	1600	430/730
		West Bank		
No immigration				
1991	0.90	115	180	0/65
2000	1.21	120	210	5/95
2020	3.67	170	460	25/215
600,000 immigrants[c]				
1991	0.90	115	180	0/65
2000	1.61	125	250	10/135
2020	3.67	170	460	55/345
		Gaza		
1991	0.60	95	140	35/80
2000	0.81	100	160	40/100
2020	1.58	120	240	60/180
Total Demand—Low Estimates (1 million Israeli, no West Bank immigrants)				
1991		2880	3100	235/455
2000		3180	3470	545/825
2020		3760	4370	1090/1725
Total Demand—High Estimates (2 million Israeli, 600,000 West Bank immigrants)				
1991		2880	3100	235/455
2000		3285	3610	640/595
2020		3990	4700	1345/2055

remain clean enough to use. Desalination plants may help solve Gaza's problem, as well as the importation of Palestinian water from the West Bank. On the other hand, the West Bank's own needs emphasize the importance of seeking an equitable and lasting solution to the hydrologic needs of the Mashreq.

Another element that must be considered is the rapid rate of urbanization in all the countries of the Middle East including the Mashreq. Table 3-2 illustrates this point. Amman is expected to grow from 1.44 million in 1990 to 2.7 million in 2010; Zarqa from 530 thousand to 999 thousand in the same period (Garber and Salameh, 1992). Tel Aviv may reach 2.28 million by the year 2000, and Damascus may increase from 2 million in 1990 to slightly more than 3 million in the following ten years (UN, *World Urbanization*, 1991). As this urbanization occurs, domestic water needs will increase at an even faster rate. Thus, in the not too distant future, an additional demand will be placed upon existing natural water supplies and the need to appropriate water from the agricultural sector will accelerate.

Table 3-2: PER CENT OF POPULATION IN URBAN AREAS IN MIDDLE EASTERN COUNTRIES 1950 AND 1990

Country/territory	1950	1990
Bahrain	64	83
Egypt	32	44
Gaza	51	94
Iran	27	57
Iraq	35	72
Israel	65	92
Jordan	35	68
Lebanon	23	84
Saudi Arabia	16	77
Syria	31	50
Turkey	21	61
UAE	25	81

Source: Omran and Roudi, 1993, Table 6, p. 20.

It also must be emphasized that there is no guarantee that population will not increase after 2020. That date is only twenty-five years in the future, but attempting to project population growth and water needs beyond that time is unrealistic. What we wish to emphasize is that an equitable, integrated, long-term as well as short-term planning strategy is critical, not only at this moment, but in the quarter century ahead.

ECONOMIC CONSIDERATIONS

Economics, with the individual as a rational maximizer of satisfaction in a world of relative scarcity, offers a useful paradigm for water conflict analysis. When deciding between several possible water development options, for example, benefit-cost analysis—an economic tool by which all of the future benefits and costs of a project are reduced to a single amount representing the net benefits in current dollars—can help determine which project would be the most beneficial.

Economic theory also provides guidelines for policy options for efficient water distribution. It argues, for example, that only when the price paid for a commodity is a reasonable reflection of the true cost, can market forces work for efficient distribution of the commodity. In the Mideast, as elsewhere, the cost of water to the user is highly subsidized, especially water earmarked for agriculture. The true cost of water would reflect all of the resource development, pumping, treatment and delivery costs of that water, most of which are not passed on to the user. In Israel alone, 20 per cent of the country's energy is used solely to move water from one place to another (Naff and Matson, 1984, 12).

Subsidized water, it is posited, leads to waste in agricultural practices, too little incentive for research and development of conservation techniques and practices, and, finally too much water being allocated to the agricultural sector as opposed to industry. Take away subsidies and allow the price to rise, and market incentives are created for both greater efficiency on the farm and a natural shift of water resources from the agricultural sector to industry, where contribution to GNP per unit of water is usually much higher. Since in each of the geographical areas discussed, between 70 per cent and 90 per cent of water use is allocated for agriculture, the savings in water could be substantial (Wishart, 1990). Thomas Naff has recommended such a shift of 35–40 per cent of agricultural water in both Israel and Jordan.[3]

If the price of water reflects the true costs of its development, and if property rights to water are clear, then a 'water market' can be established to allow buying and selling, ensuring through the 'invisible hand' of the marketplace that each unit of water is being used most efficiently. Water markets, whether national or international, can provide clear incentives for efficient use and guidelines for trades or transfers. Howe and Easter (1971) have derived the necessary conditions for economically efficient inter-basin water transfers in the United States, and Dinar and Wolf (1992) have discussed international water markets using a hypothetical Nile to Jordan basin transfer as a case-study. Zeitouni et al. (1992) discuss trading water rights in an international context, and Gonzalez and Rubio (1992) show that the amount of water to be transferred between basins in a Spanish case could be reduced if economic factors were considered as opposed to straight extrapolations of need.

Economic analysis may also create a framework for easing regional water tensions. According to Wishart (1990), 'conflicts over water rights are easier to resolve if transaction costs of resolution are lower, and if opportunities exist for improving the efficiency of water use and discovery'. In other words, if it is cheaper for people to co-operate and save water than it is to fight, they would rather co-operate.

Some other considerations which have been used in the past to enhance the potential for economic co-operation between players include:

- Recognizing that while water itself is a finite commodity, and therefore conducive only to zero-sum solutions ('distributive' or 'win-lose', in the language of Alternative Dispute Resolution—ADR), the benefits or welfare, derived from water are variable, and therefore tradable for non-zero-sum ('integrative' or 'win-win') solutions.
- Welfare can be measured basin-wide and among all the co-operating players, so that even when one player's individual welfare is not immediately enhanced by the loss of the resource, the resulting pay-offs of trade should result in the region as a whole being better off.
- Infrastructural considerations can enhance the argument for co-operation, especially when considering the variable aspects inherent to water resources. One or another of the players may have better resources to deal with fluctuating quantity or quality —

more storage potential, or better developed water treatment for example—which can help encourage an alliance.

There are, however, problems inherent in using economic theory as the tool for water conflict analysis—problems which can lead to weaknesses in the economic solutions prescribed. One problem is that water is not a pure economic good. Options to the consumer of most goods include migrating to where it is cheaper or abstaining from it altogether if the price is too high. Given small, neighbouring countries with restricted borders, migration to water sources is not a viable alternative, nor, for more obvious biologic reasons, is abstaining. Presumably, though, the analysis is restricted to water for agriculture where there is ample room for reducing demand before running into such limits.

Another problem with economic analysis is more serious because it has to do with a force much more fundamental than economic theory—that is, national emotions. All the countries on both sides of the Jordan have been built from the farm up and for the agriculturist, whether the *fellah* or the *kibbutznik*, land holds a special mystique, ergo the water serving the land. Both Arabic and Hebrew ideologies are rife with slogans of 'making the desert bloom' and 'nations rooted in their land'. In this context, water invariably becomes the 'life blood' of a nation. One result of this has been a certain leeway granted to agriculture in the area, both political, as noted previously, and economic.

One striking example of water 'diseconomy' is the case of Israeli settlements on the Golan Heights. The twenty-four, mostly agricultural settlements of the Golan have a total population of about 3500. In 1980, approximately 80 per cent of the 50 mcm/yr used by these settlements was pumped up from the Sea of Galilee—a height differential of 600 metres (Davis, 1980, p. 27; Inbar and Maos, 1984, 22). Each cubic metre of water weighs a metric ton. Were the settlers to include the costs of the energy required to lift that much water that high, their crops could not possibly be competitive. But settlements on the Golan heights are viewed as more than a source of agricultural production. They are also outposts, whose presence creates a kind of first line of defence against the Syrians.

This perceived connection between settlements and security holds true throughout the country. As Frey and Naff (1985) write:

Israeli agriculture is not merely an ordinary economic sector. It is linked to the crucial matter of settlements, and settlements are linked to defense and national security.

This is what makes Golan cotton competitive in the eyes of the Israelis. Whether or not the pricing of water will play a role in the ongoing negotiations regarding the Golan Heights remains to be seen.

Economists, especially those from outside the region, who overlook this fundamental aspect of a 'national water ethic' held by each of the countries involved, can be confounded by unanticipated recalcitrance among the players. Cal Burwell, former director of research for the proposed agro-industrial complex (Chapter 6), recently commented that, 'Some of what's valuable to the folks over there just doesn't fit into what our folks would call "good economics".'[4]

Economists increasingly recognize the overpowering non-economic values water users sometime attribute to the water which they utilize and/or need. These may include (Wolf, 1992):

- Political attributes of water, e.g., perceived past injustices, national pride
- Co-operation *per se* (e.g., the World Bank does not include international co-operation as a benefit in benefit/cost analyses (Olivares, 1986)
- Physical security
- Perceptions of beauty in the environment
- The 'land ethic'—inherent value of 'non-economic' species and landscapes
- Food or water security—the psychological value of control
- Open space

The last item represents a departure from historic economic arguments in the Middle East. In Israel, for example, water has been subsidized for years as a means of promoting population dispersion and food security. These subsidies have diminished somewhat in recent years, as the ministry of agriculture has accepted a more market oriented approach to planning. However, as population continues to soar with natural growth and extensive immigration, the suggestion has been made to increase subsidies once again as a way to preserve open space throughout the extensive developments.[5]

Additional factors often convolute the possibility for traditionally economic analysis, particularly in an international setting. These political and institutional constraints to economic co-operation include:

a) Some level of hostility between the players. Hostility can be between basins (e.g.., northern and southern California), between economic sectors (urban versus agricultural users), or, especially, between political entities (e.g., the case of the Turkish Peace Pipeline, Akdogan, 1992; Nile water transfer, Dinar and Wolf, 1992).

b) Property rights (ownership of water) are often unclear and, occasionally, bitterly contested. Although water is internally nationalized in all of the cases discussed in this work, international ownership is often unspecified.

c) State subsidized water often makes the economics of any transfer or trade unclear, as described above.

d) National prestige can be tied up in the population's perception of its water resources, decreasing the apparent desirability of co-operation. National pride in 'Israeli oranges', or 'Egyptian cotton', for example, may preclude a shift to other agricultural products or to industry, even if the former product(s) can be imported at less expense from abroad.

e) Usually, when an inter-basin or international exchange is agreed upon, it is for a specific amount to be delivered annually. Because of treaty or infrastructural limitations (such as pumping, storage, or delivery capacity), the 'solution' is discrete, and cannot be arrived at dynamically. This limits the potential for efficient water market transactions, which often rely on variable solutions (e.g., Lekakis and Giannias, 1992; Zeitouni et al., 1992).

f) Insulation from the total picture can also play its part. Negotiating teams usually include diplomats and engineers whose primary considerations are most often politics and reliable delivery, rather than economic efficiency.

Nevertheless, while recognizing such limitations, one can still use economic analysis as a useful tool to provide guidelines for increasing hydrologic efficiency. Following these guidelines can be crucial, particularly as limits on water supplies are approached. Whereas diseconomies dictated by ideology might be tolerated under conditions of water sufficiency, such diseconomies cannot continue indefinitely, especially with regard to investments under conditions of system shortages (Galnoor, 1978).

THE ENVIRONMENT

While the water supply of a country remains constant unless augmented from external sources or depleted by severe mismanagement, as discussed above, populations will steadily increase in the foreseeable future.[6] At the same time, urbanization and the 'revolution of rising expectations' assure increasing per capita water demands. The demand for more water and the search for it can have severe adverse effects on agricultural lands, forests, fisheries, and even on local communities. Therefore, any attempt to develop water resources inevitably results in some modification of the environment. This, in turn, necessitates 1) recognition of the concepts of sustainable development and resilience, 2) the adoption of a comprehensive viewpoint for planning purposes, and 3) the pursuit of greater efficiencies regarding both water consumption and the development of projects intended to augment water supplies.

In response to this issue, the assessment of the impact of water development projects on the environment has come to be recognized as an integral part of planning.[7] Water management agencies almost everywhere are conscious of the need to identify and evaluate the impact of projects on the ecological systems involved, and their many component parts. It must be recognized, however, that assessments of projects that recognize only the negative impacts, and ignore the positive ones are both incomplete and counterproductive. The old adage, 'You can't make omelettes without breaking eggs', certainly applies in this case. For example, the decline in fish stocks in the Mediterranean, so often cited as a negative impact of the High Dam on the Nile river has actually been compensated by later increases in production both in the Mediterranean and in Lake Nasser (Biswas et al., 1993, p. 49).

The situation is further complicated by the fact that while the environmental impact assessment (EIA) process has become mandatory in many industrialized countries, its actual use so far in developing countries has been slowed by the lack of operational methodology appropriate to nations with limited expertise, resources, data, and time. What is needed is the development of new guidelines that can actually be used for planning and water management in those areas. However, the search for such guidelines is often impeded by inter-ministerial rivalries which inhibit co-ordination and co-operation on an intra-mural level.

The constraints involved in the search for sustainable, environmentally correct water project development cover a broad spectrum of activities. These include:

- Debts and financial deterioration in developing countries.
- Lack of appropriate and consistent policies.
- Delays in the completion of ancillary projects (canals, etc.) after completion of major elements (e.g., dams) which slow the realization of potential benefits.
- Absence of or inadequacy of monitoring, evaluation, and feedbacks at both national and international levels.
- Lack of technical manpower and training facilities.
- Lack of beneficiary participation in planning, implementation, and operation of projects.
- Lack of knowledge, appropriate research, and incentive to use new technologies and approaches.
- Institutional weaknesses and lack of co-ordination between ministries.
- Lack of donor co-ordination which results in conflicting advice.
- Inappropriate or insufficient project development by donor agencies (e.g., irrigation development without drainage or attention to runoff disposal).

In order to meet the needs of planning for sustainable development and to counter the constraints which such a search inevitably encounters, seven sets of concepts or themes have been identified as necessary:

1) The adoption of a comprehensive viewpoint.
2) The promotion of a search for the widest possible range of choice.
3) The recognition of water as an economic good.
4) The use of the river basin as a unit of area in various phases of river management.
5) The involvement of the public in planning and policy making.
6) The assessment of social impacts.
7) The consideration of environmental impacts.

In turn, the review of such environmental impacts must include not only short-term phenomena such as migratory project workers as vectors in the spread of disease, but also long-term environmental consequences. Among the latter are impact on water quality, ground water, and on soil; the possibility of earthquakes which may result from water impoundment and seepage and/or the risk of dam failures; ground water mining; effects on climate; impact on living organisms and on human health—particularly through water related diseases (N.C. Thanh and Tam, 1990, 10–20).

In considering the natural environment within the Mashreq, little definitive research has taken place. The call for such work is increasing, but planning to date has tended to consider creating infrastructure rather than worrying about the possible negative results of such projects.

This is not a new picture. A visit to the Cedars of Lebanon reveals denuded hillsides stripped of trees, other vegetation and soil, with only what once must have been a sacred grove surviving. The question is, will the 21st century see even more devastating environmental impact, or can the water projects which are planned and anticipated be translated into some form of sustainable development? Such an open situation necessitates a broad approach to the types of environmental deterioration which have already or will soon be taking place in the Mashreq's core and periphery.

Environmentally affected areas or elements (aquifers, ponds, springs, rivers, lakes, etc.) are almost always viewed as isolated phenomena. But such a perspective is misleading. For example, a river considered environmentally has three aspects. There is the river itself and its ecology; there is the inter-action between the river and the immediate area through which it flows (Tenenbaum, 1994), and there is the river's function as a route whereby exchanges take place between widely diverse environments (i.e., from its often cool mountain headwaters to its debouchment—again often—in arid or humid tropical zones) (Dynesius and Nilsson, 1994, p. 753).

Point locations, e.g., isolated oases such as the (Al) Azraq in Jordan can serve the same functions. The Azraq oasis, before its deterioration at human hands, in addition to having its own special ecology and also serving the desert matrix in which it exists, was a major stopping point on an important migratory bird flyway between northern Asia and Africa. Whether or not its recent restoration will restore it to its original condition, including serving the purposes of avian migration, remains to be seen.

An examination of Table 3-3 reveals the diversity and inter-connectedness of the impacted and potentially impacted environments of the Mashreq.

Table 3-3: A GEOGRAPHIC SPECTRUM OF EXISTING AND
POSSIBLE WATER RELATED ENVIRONMENTAL
IMPACTS IN THE MASHREQ

Type of Pollution	Open Sea	Gulf & Inshore	Tidal Zone/ Littoral	Underground Waters Aquifers/ Groundwater
Removals				
Water	XX	XX	XX	Depletions: Saq. Syrian, Jezirah, West Bank, Jordan
Soil	XX	XX	XX	XX
Biota	Over fishing	Over fishing	XX	XX
Additions (Pollution)				
Silt	XX	Northern Gulf	Deltas	XX
Salts	Northern Gulf	Aqaba & return flow Dead zones	Desalination intrusions	Salt water
Heavy metals and Sewage, etc.	XX	Bilges	General: no nesting/ feeding grounds	e.g., Gaza
Inundations	XX	XX	XX	Waterlogging in Saudi Arabian cities
Biota	XX	XX	Bacteria	Bacteria
Visual & Acoustical	XX Oil rigs	Off-shore Desal. plants	Oil spills Flotsam & jetsam	XX

Type of Pollution	Springs & Oases	Rivers & Streams	Lakes & Reservoirs	Playas & Salt Lakes
Removals				
Water	Israeli coastal springs; Azraq Oasis	Euphrates Asi Jordan	Lake Assad	Dead sea

(*Contd.*)

Table 3.3 (contd.)

Soil	XX	Erosion	XX	XX
Biota	Azraq Oasis bird life	possible loss of spawning fish	XX	XX
Additions **(Pollution)**				
Silt & Sand	Algerian Oases overwhelmed	Euphrates	Lake Ataturk Lake Assad, etc.	XX
Salts	Possible	Euphrates Shatt Al-Arab lower Jordan	Possible	XX
Heavy Metals & Sewage, etc.	Possible	As with above salts	Possible	Possible
Inundations	XX	Runoff into Syrian Jezirah	Sea of Galilee water capacity	Possible Dead sea flooded shorelines
Biota	Bacteria	Schistosomes bacteria	New macro species schistosomes	XX
Visual & Acoustical	Desiccation	XX	Shifting shore line factories	Factories & chemical plants

The continuum of environments is listed along the table's rows, and begins with the open waters of the Mediterranean and the Red seas. These are followed by gulfs and inshore waters and tidal zones and littorals. Underground waters are listed next, including aquifers which often reach seaward beyond the tidal zone as well as appearing as springs and natural oases on land. The famous submarine fresh water springs of the Gulf, which in recent years have ceased to flow because of excessive pumping on shore, are an example of the former. Groundwater, *per se*, is closely connected both to surface seepage and flow to and from aquifers. Rivers and streams, lakes and reservoirs follow logically, as do playas and salt lakes (e.g., the Dead sea).

The columns of this table follow a similar pattern. In the final analysis environmental deterioration results from the addition or removal of substances at a rate beyond the capacity of the existing natural system to replace, or integrate, or neutralize them. Thus, removal as a general category includes water depletions or subtractions, erosion of soil and nutrients, and the destruction or diversion of biota, both flora and fauna. Pollution, conversely, means the deposition of water borne silt or wind blown materials such as salts, the precipitating of salts on irrigated lands, or the introduction of dissolved materials into nearby streams. Heavy metals and artificial contaminants such as DDT, PCBs, and petroleum derivatives also constitute polluting additions. Introduced biota represent a special category whether they are microscopic (e.g., bacteria and schistosomes) or unwanted macro-species (rabbits to Australia, zebra mussels to the Great Lakes).

Inundation as well as temporary flooding either by polluted or clean waters can also be destructive (Tenenbaum, 1994). Finally, visual and acoustical pollution can become serious problems if they destroy the tourism potential of an area, or adversely affect local residents (desalination plants near tourist beaches).

Table 3-3 shows a number of such examples. Certain cells are marked where the possibility of environmental deterioration exists. The reader undoubtedly can supply numerous additional examples.

Removals from the open seas include over-fishing and the diminishing of nutrients (a result of their entrapment in the silts of upstream reservoirs), and thereafter, the depletion of fish stocks. Additions include oil tanker spills and the flushing of bilges.[8] Another example of pollution, although the water involved may be of reasonably good quality, is the waterlogging of areas of Riyadh through excessive application of irrigation water. On the other hand, the excessive removal of water for irrigation may seriously deplete the Euphrates river in the near future. Even the Dead sea, as this text indicates elsewhere, is either perilously low, or in future danger of over-filling, depending upon the viewpoint of the observer.

Thus, the environmental assessments of a Med-Dead or Red-Dead canal need to be complete and rigorous (Wolf, 1992). The Aqaba pumped-storage scheme will have less environmental impact if a wastewater treatment system is incorporated into the regional development plan. But the environmental dangers in this case would come not only directly from the movement of saltwater through fragile desert eco-systems and unregulated return flow to the Gulf of Aqaba, but also indirectly, from population moving to sites offering new opportunities and the impact of the infrastructure necessary to serve such groups.

The major environmental concerns with desalination have to do with the waste heat and air pollution in energy generation. Appropriate methods for disposing of the brine, which is an inevitable by-product of the process and which can be a hazard to delicate marine eco-systems, must also be considered. No serious consideration of controlling related air pollution has come to the attention of these authors.[9]

Another issue which should be raised with large-scale reliance on desalination is the question of coastal aesthetics. Most large-scale desalination plants currently produce to the tune of 20,000–40,000 m^3/day of sweet water. If Israel were to try to de-salt 400 mcm/yr., as some have suggested, this would require between 27 and 55 large-scale plants. At perhaps 1/2 kilometre of coast necessary for each plant, this would require dedicating between 13 and 27 kilometres of prime coastal land to nothing but desalination. The visual impact of such plants as viewed from pristine, recreational beaches might have a deleterious effect upon the tourism potential of the coast.

Other hazards relate to the possible Med-Dead or Red-Dead canal schemes. These include the unknown consequences of mixing water from two chemically distinct sources and what chemical reactions and precipitates may result (Ross, 1983). Questions like these will have to be answered before the Dead sea project's implementation. This list might be extended into volumes, but our intention here is to emphasize the necessity of maintaining a holistic point of view during the planning process.

CONCLUSIONS

This prognostication need not be entirely one of gloom and doom. One clear environmental benefit of a canal project would be the restoration of the Dead sea to its historic level. Without such a project, the Dead sea will continue to shrink and its level drop. Although not much wildlife is affected (except for bacteria, the Dead sea is appropriately named), potash works and health resorts on both shores will continue to contend with the inconvenience and costs of an increasingly distant shoreline. With inflow from either the Mediterranean or the Red sea, the Dead sea would be restored to its historic level in about twenty years.[10] In another example, the 'Jordan Valley Peace/Salt Drainage Canal' (see below) should be designed to protect the fresh water environment and eco-system of the lower Jordan, and be given high priority in the water master plan (shown in Table 3-3).

The deterioration of Jordan's Azraq oasis has been mentioned earlier. The oasis has now been restored to much of its former verdure by means of a reclamation programme recently carried out under the direction of Dr Ghaith Fariz of the University of Jordan. Through careful monitoring of the water supply in Amman, periods of low urban water use have been identified during which reverse pumping from the city to the oasis helps create equilibrium between the two areas. But even when positive steps are taken, the need for vigilance regarding the environment remains important. The question persists, can such restoration endure in the face of long-term population growth?

The true import of this chapter's discussion will become apparent only as planners, diplomats, and engineers attempt to forge a lasting, equitable, and environmentally sustainable peace. The environment must remain clean and hospitable. Population increase is an *eminence gris* to be dealt with. Economics represent the key that must be fashioned to unlock the door to peace which population and environment define.

NOTES

1. Waste disposal (i.e., human sewage) requires significant amounts of water. In most situations where flush toilets are available potable water from a single domestic system is used. Under ideal circumstances, gray water or salt water would be substituted.
2. This question is undeniably rendered very difficult because of the national perceptions and symbolic behaviour discussed in Chapter 1.
3. Lecture delivered at University of Wisconsin, Madison, in March 1990.
4. Interview, February 1990.
5. Interview, Martin Sherman, Economist, Ministry of Agriculture, Israel, November 1991.
6. A less certain but ominous constraint is the role played by climatic factors such as global warming (See Issar, 1995).
7. The following discussion is derived from Biswas, 1993.
8. It should be noted, that the Mediterranean Sea and the Arabian/Persian Gulf are natural waste traps where inflowing surface currents which

compensate for high evaporation from the enclosed bodies of water carry in all manner of detritus (e.g., tar balls and styrofoam cigarette filters) which is trapped by the lack of return surface currents.

9. The closure and depth of the Dead Sea valley may form a natural atmospheric trap. The possibility of this should be investigated along with other environmental impasse questions.

10. The amount of inflow would then be pared back to equal the natural evaporation rate.

11 a. Projections assume constant demand for agriculture growth to come through technology; low demand assumes urban use grows at current per capita usage; high demand allows 100 cubic metres per capita for urban use.

b. Projected deficit equals annual natural potential minus projected demand.

c. Assumes 1 million immigrants to Israel by 1993, 2 million by 2000; Palestinian immigration is assumed to be between 1995 and 2005, all to the West Bank.

Part Two

Hydro-planning for Peace

4 From Hydro-conflict to Hydro-co-operation

BACKGROUND

The broad strokes outlining the preceding picture of conflict and co-operation provide a background for further examination of the hydro-diplomacy taking place in the Middle East. The Jordan river basin has remained the focus of such activity over several decades. Similar efforts regarding the waters of Nile, the Euphrates and Tigris, the Litani, and the Asi (Orontes) are either pending or continuing, each occupying its place in the regional picture. While each basin has its own history of competition and negotiation regarding water, this chapter focuses upon recent developments between Israel and its Arab neighbours in their quest for adequate water supplies.

By 1991, several events combined to shift the emphasis on the potential for 'hydro-conflict' in the Middle East to the potential for 'hydro-co-operation'. The first event was natural, but limited to the Jordan basin. Three years of below-average rainfall caused a dramatic tightening in the water management practices of each of the riparians —Israel, Jordan, Lebanon, Palestinians,[1] and Syria—including rationing, cut-backs to agriculture by as much as 30 per cent, and restructuring of water pricing and allocations. Most water decision-makers agree that these steps, particularly regarding pricing practices and allocations to agriculture, were long overdue. Such actions imposed short-term hardships on those affected, but also showed that, during years of normal rainfall, there is still some flexibility in the system.

The next series of events were geo-political and region-wide. The Gulf War in 1991 and the collapse of the Soviet Union caused a realignment of political alliances in the Middle East, events which finally made possible the first public, face-to-face peace talks between the Arabs and the Israelis, in Madrid on 30 October, 1991. During the bilateral negotiations between Israel and each of its neighbours, it was agreed that a second series of talks[2] be established for multilateral negotiations on five subjects deemed 'regional'. Among the topics was that of water resources.

THE PROBLEM

Until the current Arab–Israeli peace negotiations began in 1991, attempts at Middle East conflict resolution always had approached political and resource problems separately. By separating the two realms of 'high' and 'low' politics, some have argued, each process was doomed to fail.[3] In all the water resource issues addressed—•the Johnston Negotiations of the mid-1950s, attempts at 'water-for-peace' through nuclear desalination in the late 1960s, negotiations over the Yarmouk river in the 1970s and 1980s, and the Global Water Summit Initiative of groundwater was separated from the political differences between the parties.[4] The above negotiations all failed to one degree or another.

While political tensions have precluded any comprehensive agreement over the waters of the Middle East, unilateral development in each country has tried to keep pace with the water needs of growing populations and economies. As a result, demand for water resources in most of the countries in the region exceeds at least 90 per cent of the renewable supply. The only exceptions to this are Lebanon and Turkey. All of the countries and territories riparian to the Jordan river —Israel, Syria, Jordan, and the West Bank (Palestine)—currently use between 95 per cent and more than 100 per cent of their annual renewable freshwater supply.[5] Gaza exceeds its renewable supplies by 50 per cent every year, resulting in serious saltwater intrusion. In recent dry years, water consumption throughout the region has routinely exceeded annual supply, the difference usually being made up through overdraft of fragile ground water systems.

In water systems as tightly managed and exploited as those of the Middle East, any future unilateral development is likely to be extremely expensive if based on technology, or politically volatile if threatening the resources of a neighbour. It has been clear to water managers for years that the most viable options include regional co-operation as a minimum prerequisite.[6]

ATTEMPTS AT CONFLICT MANAGEMENT

Since the opening session of the multilateral talks[7] in Moscow in January 1992, the Working Group on Water Resources, with the United States as 'gavel-holder,' has been the forum through which problems of water supply, demand, and institutions have been raised among the parties to the bilateral talks—Israel, Jordan, and the Palestinians (with the exception of Lebanon and Syria). Talks have also taken place among Arab states from the Maghreb including Algeria, Mauritania, Morocco and Tunisia, and from the Gulf and Red Sea: Bahrain, Egypt, Kuwait, Oman, Qatar, Saudi Arabia, the United Arab Emirates and Yemen. Participating in the talks are also 'non-regional delegations', including representatives from governments such as Canada, China, the European Union, Japan, and Turkey; and from donor NGOs such as the World Bank.[8]

The two series of the current negotiations, the bilateral and the multilateral, are designed explicitly not only to close the gap between issues of politics and issues of regional development, but perhaps to use progress on each to help catalyze the pace of the other in a positive feedback loop. The goal of both is to achieve 'a just and lasting peace in the Middle East'. The multilateral working groups are intended to provide fora for relatively free dialogues on the future of the region, and in the process, to allow inter-personal relationships to form and confidence building to take place. Decisions are made through consensus only. Given the role of the Working Group on Water Resources in this context, the objectives thus far have been more in the nature of fact-finding and workshops, rather than tackling the difficult hydro-political issues of water rights and allocations, or the development of specific projects.

The Working Group on Water has met five times (Table 4-1 and Table 4-3). The pace of success of each round has fluctuated but, in general, has been increasing. The 'second' round, the first of the water group alone, has been characterized as, 'contentious', with initial posturing on all sides. Palestinians and Jordanians, then part of a joint delegation, first raised the issue of water rights, claiming that no progress can be made on any other issue until past grievances are addressed. In sharp contrast, the Israeli position has been that water rights is a bilateral issue, and that the multilateral working group should focus on joint management and development of new resources.

Since decisions are made by consensus, little progress was made on either of these issues. Nevertheless, plans were made for continuation of the talks, an achievement in itself.

Table 4-1: MEETINGS OF THE MULTILATERAL WORKING
GROUP ON WATER RESOURCES

	Dates	Location
Multilateral organizational meeting[13]	28–9 January 1992	Moscow
Water Talks, Round 2	14–15 May 1992	Vienna
Water Talks, Round 3	16–17 September 1992	Washington, DC
Water Talks, Round 4	27–9 April 1993	Geneva
Water Talks, Round 5	26–8 October 1993	Beijing
Water Talks, Round 6	17–19 April 1994	Muscat

Table 4-2: REGIONAL TRAINING ACTION PLAN

Water Sector Level Courses
1. Concepts of integrated water resources planning and management
2. Water resources assessment, planning and management
3. Water quality management
4. Data collection and management systems
5. Alternatives in water resources development
6. Principles and applications of international water law

Water Sub-sector Level Courses
7. Management of municipal water supply systems
8. Rehabilitation of municipal water supply systems
9. Management of wastewater collection and treatment systems
10. Development of efficient irrigation systems

Specialized Courses
11. Environmental impact assessment techniques
12. Groundwater modeling
13. Public awareness campaigns for the water sector
14. Development, management and delivery of training programmes in the water sector

Table 4-3: CHRONOLOGY OF WATER-NEGOTIATION-
RELATED-EVENTS

30 October 1991	First public, face-to-face peace talks between Arabs and Israelis are held in Madrid. Talks begin as bilateral, between Israel and each of its neighbours.
28–9 January 1992	Multilateral organizational meeting in Moscow. Peace process is designed along two tracks—the bilateral negotiations, involving separate direct negotiations between Israel and each of its neighbours, and the multilateral negotiations revolving around five regional subjects, including water resources. Goal is to allow framework for defining future of the region, as well as to include peripheral Arab states, other countries, and donor NGOs.
14–15 May 1992	First meeting of Multilateral Working Group on Water Resources in Vienna (dubbed the 'second' round of multilaterals). Little practical progress made due to venting and posturing on all sides. Palestinians and Jordanians first raise issue of water rights; Israel's position is that water rights are a bilateral issue. World Bank asks each party to compile a programme for regional water resources development, following three possible scenarios: no outside investment, current government plans, and unlimited resources. These scenarios would be examined in the US for any commonalties which could be culled to induce cooperation. Only decision reached is to plan for next round of talks.
16–17 September 1992	Third round of water talks in Washington, DC. Agreement on four general subjects for multilateral talks on water: enhancement of water data, water management practices, enhancement of water supply, and concepts for regional co-operation and management. Role of multilaterals clarified to plan for future region at peace, not to implement specific agreements.
27–9 April 1993	The fourth working group on water meeting in Geneva proves difficult following a disagreement over a Palestinian request that water rights be included in multilateral talks, otherwise the Palestinians would boycott inter-sessional activities.
May 1993	Israelis and Palestinians agree to discuss water rights in the Occupied Territories within the framework of the bilateral negotiations and Palestinians agree to participate in inter-sessional activities. This agreement, which came about in discussions at the working group on refugees meeting in Oslo, also called for American representatives of the water working group to visit the region.

15 September 1993	Declaration of Principles signed between Israelis and Palestinians, which includes several water-related items, including the creation of a Palestinian Water Administration Authority and a Water Development Programme. The Programme would include investigations of development of regional agricultural and desalination projects, and a Med-Dead canal (Gaza).
26–8 October 1993	Fifth round of Working Group on Water Resources meets in Beijing. Presentations are made in each of four topics and several projects are agreed to; priority needs assessment is presented and courses are approved.
17–19 April 1994	Sixth round of Working Group meets in Muscat, Oman. The meeting is productive after all parties agree to welcome a Palestinian announcement of the creation of a Palestinian Water Authority in the autonomous territories of Gaza and Jericho (Israel agrees provided it will not be seen as a precedent in other territories). Other endorsements include: an Omani proposal to establish a desalination research and technology centre; an Israeli proposal to lead an effort of water conservation and rehabilitation of municipal water systems; a German offer to study regional supply and demand; a US proposal to perform a study of wastewater treatment and reuse; and the US and EU would implement a regional water training programme to begin in June 1994.
7–9 June 1994	Bilateral talks take place between Israel and Jordan in Washington DC. Sub-agenda items are determined for talks leading to a Treaty of Peace, including several water-related topics.
26 October 1994	Treaty of Peace signed between the Hashemite Kingdom of Jordan and the State of Israel. The treaty includes several water related items on the development of the Yarmouk river, the Jordan river, brackish water desalination in Beit'shean, and brackish ground water desalination near Araba.
28 September 1995	Interim Agreement signed between Israel and the Palestinians, broadening the autonomous zone in the West Bank to major population areas, and recognizing Palestinian water rights to be specified in future negotiations.

The third round in Washington DC in September, 1992 made somewhat more progress. Consensus was reached on a general emphasis for the watersheds that the US Department of State had proposed in May, focusing on four subjects:

- enhancement of water data.

- water management practices.
- enhancement of water supply.
- concepts for regional co-operation and management.

Progress was also made on the definition of the relationship between the multilateral and bilateral tracks. By this third meeting, it became clear that regional water-sharing agreements, or any political agreements surrounding water resources, would not be dealt with in the multilateral talks, but that the role of these talks was to deal with non-political issues of mutual concern, thereby strengthening the bilateral track. The goal for the working group on water resources became to plan for a future region at peace, and to leave the pace of implementation to the bilaterals. This distinction between 'planning' and 'implementation' became crucial, with progress only being made as the boundary between the two was continuously pushed and blurred by the mediators.

The fourth round in Geneva in April 1993 proved particularly contentious, threatening at points to grind to a halt. Initially, the meeting seemed somewhat innocuous. Proposals were made for a series of inter-sessional activities surrounding the four subjects agreed to at the previous meeting. These activities, including study tours and water-related courses, would help capacity building (i.e., greater expertise) within the region while fostering better personal and professional relations between negotiators.

The issue of water rights was raised again, however, with the Palestinians threatening to boycott the inter-sessional activities. The Jordanians, however, who had already agreed to discuss water rights with the Israelis in their bilateral negotiations, helped work out a similar arrangement on behalf of the Palestinians. Settlement of the problem was not reached at that time, but both sides eventually agreed, after quiet negotiations in May during the meeting of the working group on refugees in Oslo.

The agreement called for three Israeli–Palestinian working groups within the bilateral negotiations, one of which would deal with water rights. The Palestinians also agreed to participate in the inter-sessional activities. In addition, the US representatives on the working group were called upon to visit the region. While some expected the visiting US representatives to take the opportunity to present a strong pro-active position on the issue of water rights, the delegates insisted that any specific initiatives would have to come from the parties themselves, and that agreement would have to be by consensus.

By July 1993, the inter-sessional activities had begun, with about twenty activities as diverse as a study tour of the Colorado river basin and a series of seminars on semi-arid lands which have since taken place. Recent emphasis has been on capacity building in the region. A series of fourteen courses for participants from the region has recently been designed by the US and the EU. These range in length from two weeks to twelve months and cover subjects as broad as concepts of integrated water management and as detailed as ground-water flow modelling.

Following a June 1993 agreement in the multilaterals on a joint US/EC proposal to conduct a regional training needs assessment in the Middle East water sector, a team of specialists developed a Priority Regional Training Action Plan. The plan included a series of fourteen courses offered to managers and professionals from the region over two years beginning in June 1994. The courses were endorsed at the fifth round of water talks in Oman in April 1994. The first course which explored concepts of integrated water resources planning and management, was held in Florida. The approved courses, which range in duration from two weeks to two years are shown in Table 4-2.

On 15 September 1993, the Declaration of Principles on Interim Self-Government Arrangements was signed between Palestinians and Israelis. The declaration defined Palestinian autonomy and the re-deployment of Israeli forces out of Gaza and Jericho. Among other issues, it also called for the creation of a Palestinian Water Administration Authority. Moreover, the first item in Annex III, on co-operation in economic and development programmes, included a focus on:

Co-operation in the field of water, including a Water Development Programme prepared by experts from both sides, which will also specify the mode of co-operation in the management of water resources in the West Bank and Gaza Strip, and will include proposals for studies and plans on water rights of each party, as well as on the equitable utilization of joint water resources for implementation in and beyond the interim period.

Annex IV describes regional development programmes for co-operation, including:

- the development of a joint Israeli-Palestinian-Jordanian Plan for co-ordinated exploitation of the Dead sea area;

- the Mediterranean sea (Gaza) - Dead sea canal;
- regional desalinization and other water development projects;
- a regional plan for agricultural development, including a co-ordinated regional effort for the prevention of desertification.

The Declaration of Principles also included a description of the mechanisms by which disputes might be resolved. Article XV describes these mechanisms:

1. Disputes arising out of the application or interpretation of this Declaration of Principles, or any subsequent agreements pertaining to the interim period, shall be resolved by negotiations through a Joint Liaison Committee to be established.
2. Disputes which cannot be settled by negotiations may be resolved by a mechanism of conciliation to be agreed upon by the parties.
3. The parties may agree to submit to arbitration disputes relating to the interim period, which cannot be settled through conciliation. To this end, upon the agreement of both parties, the parties will establish an Arbitration Committee.

Although the declaration was seen as a positive development by most parties, minor consternation was expressed by the Jordanians about the Israeli-Palestinian agreement to investigate a possible Med-Dead canal (per Uri Shamir 6/94). In the working group on regional economic development, the Italians had pledged $2.5 million towards a study of a Red-Dead canal as a joint Israeli-Jordanian project; building both would not be feasible. The Israelis pointed out in private conversations with the Jordanians that all possible projects should be investigated, and only then could rational decisions on implementation be made.

The Declaration of Principles, although a bilateral agreement, helped streamline some logistically awkward aspects of the multi-laterals, by making the PLO openly responsible for the talks and separating the Palestinian delegations from the Jordanians.

By the fifth round of water talks in Beijing in October 1993, a routine of sorts seemed to be established. Reports were presented on each of the four topics agreed to at the second meeting in Vienna—enhancement of data availability; enhancing water supply; water management and conservation; and concepts of regional co-operation and management—and a new series of inter-sessional activities was announced.

THE OUTCOME

By the end of the fifth round of talks, the following agreements had been reached:

1. Enhancement of Data Availability
   * agreement on the need for regional data banks (banks, plural) because of Egypt (per Lawson 7/94),
   * a workshop would be held at USGS facilities in Atlanta as would additional workshops on the subject as part of the US-EU Priority Training Needs Assessment;
   * a workshop on the standardization of methodologies and formats for data collection would be held.

2. Enhancing Water Supply
   * feasibility studies are being conducted on facilities for the desalination of brackish water, by Japan in Jordan and by the EU in Gaza;
   * Canada compiled an exhaustive literature review on water technologies;
   * Oman's suggestion was accepted to conduct a survey on the current status of desalination research and technology;
   * a Canadian proposal for the installation of a rainwater catchment system in Gaza was accepted, marking the first concrete project to be accepted by the working group;

3. Water Management and Conservation
   * Austria ran a seminar on water technologies in arid and semi-arid regions, with special reference to the Middle East;
   * the US organized two seminars jointly sponsored by the water and environment working groups, one on the treatment of wastewater in small communities, and one on dry lands agriculture;
   * the World Bank is carrying out surveys of water conservation in the West Bank, Gaza, and Jordan.[9]

4. Regional Co-operation and Management
   * the UN is organizing a seminar on various models for regional co-operation and management;
   * the US is planning a workshop on weather forecasting;

- Jordan proposed that the working group define a 'water charter' for the Middle East, to define the principles of regional co-operation and determine mechanisms for water conflict resolution. The proposal was not adopted.

The sixth round of talks was held in Muscat, Oman in April 1994, the first of the water talks to be held in an Arab country, and the first of any working group to be held in the Gulf. Tensions mounted immediately before the talks as it became clear that the Palestinians would use the occasion as a platform to announce the appointment of a Palestinian National Water Authority. While such an authority was called for in the Declaration of Principles, possible responses to both its unilateral nature and to the appropriateness of the working group as the proper forum for the announcement was unclear. Only a flurry of activity prior to the talks guaranteed that the announcement would be welcomed by all parties. This agreement set the stage for a particularly productive meeting. In two days, the working group endorsed:

- an Omani proposal to establish a desalination research and technology centre in Muscat, which would support regional co-operation in desalination research among all interested parties. This marked the first Arab proposal to reach consensus in the working group;
- an Israeli proposal to rehabilitate and make more efficient water systems in small-sized communities in the region. This was the first Israeli proposal to be accepted by any working group;
- a German proposal to study the water supply and demand development among interested core parties in the region;
- a US proposal to develop wastewater treatment and re-use facilities for small communities at several sites in the region. The proposal was jointly sponsored by the water and environmental working groups;
- implementation of the US/EU regional training programme, as described in Table 4-2.

As mentioned above, the working group officially welcomed the announcement of the creation of the Palestinian Water Authority, and pledged to work with the authority on multilateral water issues. Recent progress has been made in bilateral negotiations, both between Jordan and Israel and between Israel and the Palestinians. On 7 June 1994, the two states announced that they had reached an agreement on a sub-agenda for co-operation, building on an agenda for peace talks which had been agreed to on 14 September 1993, which would lead eventually to a peace treaty. This sub-agenda included several water-related items, notably in the first heading listed (in advance of security issues, and border and territorial matters),

Group A—Water, Energy, and the Environment

I. Surface water basins.
   a. Negotiation of mutual recognition of the rightful water allocations of the two sides in Jordan river and Yarmouk river waters with mutually acceptable quality.
   b. Restoration of water quality in the Jordan river below Lake Tiberius to usable standards.
   c. Protection of water quality.

II. Shared groundwater aquifers.
   a. Renewable fresh water aquifers—southern area between the Dead Sea and the Red Sea.
   b. Fossil aquifers—area between the Dead Sea and the Red Sea.
   c. Protection of the water quality of both.

III. Alleviation of water shortage.
   a. Development of water resources.
   b. Municipal water shortages.
   c. Irrigation water shortages.

IV. Potentials of future bilateral co-operation, within a regional context where appropriate.
   [Includes Red Sea-Dead Sea canal; management of water basins; and inter-disciplinary activities in water, environment and energy.]

On 26 October 1994 Israel and Jordan formalized a peace treaty after resolving the last and most contentious issue, shared water resources.
   According to Annex II of the accord:

Israel will limit its withdrawals from the Yarmouk to 25 mcm/yr. Jordan has rights to the rest of the normal flow of the river plus 10 mcm/yr desalinated brackish spring water (out of a total of 20 mcm/yr to be desalinated);

Jordan will effectively store 20 mcm/yr of winter floodwater in Israel by allowing Israel to pump it from the Yarmouk in the winter months and having it returned from the Jordan in the summer. Floodwater in addition to current uses will be split between the two countries;

Two dams will be constructed—one each on the Yarmouk and the Jordan (Israel can use up to 3 mcm/yr of increased storage capacity).

Israel can expand by 10 mcm/yr pumping of ground water wells in the Arava/Araba, which according to the redefined border now fall within Jordanian territory.

An additional 50 mcm/yr will be developed through joint projects, to be determined by a Joint Water Committee;

The Joint Water Committee, comprised of three members from each country, will also collect relevant data on water resources, specify work procedures and details, and form specialized sub-committees, as needed.

Bilateral agreement has been forthcoming between Israel and the Palestinians as well. Between 1993 and 1995, Israeli and Palestinian representatives negotiated to broaden the 'Declaration of Principles' to encompass greater West Bank territory. On 28 September 1995, the 'Israeli-Palestinian Interim Agreement on the West Bank and the Gaza Strip', nicknamed 'Oslo II', was signed in Washington DC. The question of water rights was one of the most difficult to negotiate with a final agreement postponed to be included in the negotiations for final status arrangements. Nevertheless, tremendous compromise was achieved between the two sides. Israel recognized the Palestinian claim to water rights—of an amount to be determined in final status negotiations—and a Joint Water Committee was established to co-operatively manage West Bank water and to develop new supplies.

According to the agreement, Israeli forces are scheduled to withdraw from six Palestinian cities in order from north to south, and from 450 towns and villages throughout the West Bank. The final status of Israeli settlements in the West Bank has yet to be determined. No territory whatsoever was identified as being necessary for Israeli annexation due to access to water resources, as some had predicted. In fact, the second and third cities scheduled for Israeli withdrawal—Tulkarm and Kalkilya—fall well within the 'red line' delineated in Israeli studies as being necessary to retain for water security.

OBSERVATIONS

Given the length of time that the region has been enmeshed in bitter conflict, the pace of accomplishment of the peace process has been impressive, no less so in the area of water resources. This may be due in part to the structure of the peace talks, with the two complementary and mutually reinforcing tracks—the bilateral and the multilateral. As noted earlier, past attempts at resolving water issues separate from their political framework, dating from the early 1950's through 1991, all failed to one degree or another. Once the taboo of Israelis and Arabs meeting openly in face-to-face talks was broken in Madrid in October 1991, the floodgates were open, as it were, and a flurry of long-repressed activity on water resources began to take place outside of the official peace process. This included several academic conferences on Middle Eastern water resources in, among other places, Canada, Turkey, Illinois, Washington DC (3) and, notably, the first Israeli-Palestinian conference on water resources in Geneva; unofficial 'track II' dialogues in Cairo, New Mexico, and Idaho; the establishment by the IWRA of the 'Middle East Water Commission' (responsible for this volume) to help facilitate research on the subject, and organization of the Middle East Water Information Network (MEWIN) to co-ordinate regional data collection.

While this flurry of water-related activity may have been moderately helpful in generating ideas outside the constraints of the official process, and more so in fostering better personal relations between the water professional of the region, many negotiators involved with the official process suggest that it has had limited influence. This is because as yet no mechanism exists to encourage dialogue between the tracks.[10]

Despite the relative success of the multilateral working group on water, and given its stated objective to deal with non-political issues of mutual concern, one might wonder where the process might go from there.[11] The working group has performed admirably in the crucial early stages of negotiations as a vehicle for venting past grievances, presenting various views of the future, and, perhaps most important, allowing for personal 'de-demonization' and confidence-building on which the future regional peace will be built.

Currently, however, there is some frustration on the part of many of the participants that it is not, by design, a vehicle for actually resolving any of the conflicting issues. The contentious topics of water rights and allocations, which some argue must be solved before proceeding with any cooperative projects, are relegated to the bilateral negotiations, where they take a relatively lower priority. Likewise, the principles of integrated watershed management are difficult to encourage: water quantity, quality, and rights all fall within the purview of different negotiating frameworks—the working group on water, the working group on the environment, and the various bilateral negotiations, respectively.[12] Finally, and perhaps somewhat related, are the limitations imposed by Syrian and Lebanese refusal to participate in any of the multilateral working groups. The result of this omission means that a comprehensive settlement of the conflicts related to the Jordan or Yarmouk rivers is precluded from discussion.

The question, therefore, arises whether a new track for a water dialogue may be useful, one falling between the regional support role of the multilateral working group and the narrow political focus of the bilateral negotiations. Perhaps a watershed-wide meeting would be helpful—for example, an Israel/Jordan/Syria group on the problems of the Yarmouk basin. Such dialogues could address all of the water-related problems of each watershed, including water rights, quantity, and quality. The focus might be broadened over time until it overlaps with the current multilateral working group to become a true regional water authority. By the same token, watershed dialogues relating to peripheral river basins—the Euphrates with Turkey, Syria and Iraq—would enhance questions of sources of water external to the core area as they relate to region-wide peace.

NOTES

1. We recognize the validity of the term 'Palestine' (see footnote 1, Chapter 1), but at the time referred to for this usage Palestine was recognized by Palestinians, but had little international usage, *per se*.

2. The word 'series' is used in this context to distinguish these formal activities from those often referred as 'second track diplomacy' wherein informal, low profile meetings between negotiators are arranged by 'honest brokers'. Such meetings are intended to establish interpersonal relations and to allow the airing of topics without the constraints of national position taking.

3. For particularly cogent presentations of this argument, *see*, Lowi, Miriam. *Water and Power: The Politics of a Scarce Resource in the*

Jordan River Basin. Cambridge: Cambridge University Press, 1993; and Waterbury, John. 'Transboundary Water and the Challenge of International Co-operation in the Middle East'. Presented at a symposium on Water in the Arab World, Harvard University, 1–3 October 1993.

4. For more details of these issues in the region's hydro-political history, *see* Wolf, A. *Hydropolitics Along the Jordan River: The Impact of Scarce Water Resources on the Arab-Israeli Conflict*. Tokyo: United Nations University Press, 1995.

5. For the hydrography of the region, *see* Kolars, John. 'Water Resources of the Middle East.' *Canadian Journal of Development Studies*. 1992.

6. *See*, for example, Biswas, A. et al., (ed.) *Water for Sustainable Development*. Oxford: Oxford University Press, 1993; and Lonergan, Stephen C. and David B. Brooks. *Parting the Waters: The Role of Freshwater in the Israeli-Arab Conflict*. Ottawa: International Development and Research Centre, 1994.

7. For an excellent description of the multilateral working groups in the context of the bilateral peace talks, *see*, Peters, Joel. *Building Bridges: The Arab-Israeli Multilateral Talks*. London: The Royal Institute of International Affairs, 1994.

8. The complete list of parties invited to each round includes representatives from: Algeria, Australia, Austria, Bahrain, Belgium, Canada, China, Denmark, European Union, Egypt, Finland, France, Germany, Greece, India, Ireland, Israel, Italy, Japan, Jordan, Kuwait, Luxembourg, Mauritania, Morocco, Netherlands, Norway, Oman, Palestine, Portugal, Qatar, Russia, Saudi Arabia, Spain, Sweden, Switzerland, Tunisia, Turkey, Ukraine, United Arab Emirates, United Kingdom, United Nations, United States, the World Bank, and Yemen.

9. This has been done. For more information, *see* The World Bank. 'Water Conservation in the Occupied Territories'. Washington DC, April 1994.

10. The term 'Track II' refers to those activities outside of the official negotiations. There may be some confusion, because in the case of the Middle East peace talks, the official process is likewise divided in two—the bilateral negotiations and the multilateral working groups.

11. Biswas makes the argument for the systematic analyses of international water conflicts in, Biswas, Asit. 'Indus Water Treaty: The Negotiating Process'. *Water International* 17 (1992).

12. There is slightly more overlap than the institutional setting might indicate. Several of the regional delegates sit on both bilateral and multilateral groups, and each of the states have some sort of steering committee which fosters communication. Furthermore, the US team includes members who participate in both the water and the environment

working groups, which helps ensure that issues of water quantity and quality are not entirely separated.

13. After some confusion in numbering, it was eventually officially decided that the multilateral organizational meeting in Moscow represented the first round of the multilateral working groups. Subsequent meetings are therefore numbered correspondingly, beginning with two.

5 Techno-Political Decision-making for Water Resources Development in the Jordan River Watershed

The accord between Israel and the Palestine Liberation Organization (PLO) in Oslo on 13 September 1993, produced a Declaration of Principles which included proposals for an inter-state regional economic development plan (Israel/PLO, 1993). Regional economic development was conceived or as a key element in sustaining the peace process in the region. Similarly, regional watershed development was emphasized in an agenda for co-operation, signed between Jordan and Israel in June, 1994.

This chapter examines regional water-energy development alternatives considering both technical and political aspects of viability. Our considerations are in the context of sharing resources and benefits, taking into account the next possible multilateral peace agreement among Israel, Palestine, and Jordan. Syria, Lebanon, Egypt and Saudi Arabia could also share resources and benefits from some of these schemes.

WATER AND ENERGY: KEY ISSUES OF REGIONAL DEVELOPMENT

Hydro-Political Positions[1]

Before investigating specific projects, the major hydro-political issues facing each political entity are examined:

Israeli water issues

Sustainable yield of renewable fresh waters in Israel is approximately $1,500 \times 10^6$ m^3 per annum. Israel had already exceeded this level by the early 1970s, and had to cut 29 per cent from its national water budget from $1,987 \times 10^6$ m^3 in 1987 to $1,420 \times 10^6$ m^3 in 1991 due to severe drought. Israel accomplished this without losing net agricultural product or economic growth. Overall water savings in the agricultural sector were 39 per cent during the same period—from $1,434 \times 10^6$ m^3 in 1986 to 875×10^6 m^3 in 1991. Israel feels confident that it can continue to meet its own needs—perhaps with additional desalination plants—but also feels that it cannot relinquish any sizeable portion of the water it already uses.

Palestinian water issues

Israel took control of the West Bank in 1967, including the recharge areas for aquifers which flow west and north-west into Israel (at about 320×10^6 m^3/yr and 140×10^6 m^3/yr respectively) and east to the Jordan valley (about 125×10^6 m^3/yr). The entire renewable recharge of these first two aquifers is already being exploited and the third is close to being depleted. Total consumption within the West Bank is 35×10^6 m^3/yr, mostly from wells, for Israeli settlements (population 125,000); and 118×10^6 m^3/yr, from wells and cisterns, for some 1,200,000 Palestinians (Table 5-1, Table 5-2, Table 5-3).[2] Israel is dependent on the West Bank for a total of 430×10^6 m^3 per annum of its water supply out of a total $1,420 \times 10^6$ m^3, which accounts for 30 per cent of its annual water potential. Because any overdraft would result in saltwater intrusion along Israel's coastal plain, or eventually even into the mountain aquifers, Palestinian water usage has been severely limited by the Israeli authorities. Palestinians, on the other hand, have claimed first rights to all of the ground and surface water which originates on the West Bank, and have objected to Israeli controls. Palestinians were also to receive $70–170 \times 10^6$ m^3/yr from the Jordanian share of the Johnston negotiations of 1953–5, but to date have not.

Gaza is probably the most hydrographically desperate political entity in the region. Completely dependent on the 60×10^6 m^3/yr of annual groundwater recharge, Gazans currently use approximately 95×10^6 m^3/yr. The difference between annual supply and use is made up by over-pumping in the shallow coastal aquifer, resulting in dangerous salt-water intrusion of existing wells and ever-decreasing per capita water availability, which is already the lowest in the region.

Jordanian water issues

Jordan will very soon exceed its renewable fresh water resources of 870 $\times 10^6$ m³/yr. Only two major tributaries of the Jordan river system have not been fully developed—Wadi Mujib, with an annual flow of 78×10^6 m³, and the Yarmouk, with annual flood flows of 168×10^6 m³ (World Bank, 1988). Wadi Mujib, which is the third largest tributary flowing into the Dead sea, has no inter-state riparian complications as does the Yarmouk. One current question on sustainable water development in Jordan is whether it can afford to continue to develop fossil groundwater in deep sandstone aquifers, like the Disi, and if so, then 'for what'? and 'for how long'? These questions are critical, for the Disi is shared with Saudi Arabia (known as the Saq) and shows signs of rapid depletion.

ENERGY-WATER ISSUES

Energy issues relating to water resources are critical matters in the development of non-oil producing countries like Israel, Palestine, and Jordan. These countries are major riparians of the overburdened Jordan river system, and all have increasing demand for desalination and the treatment and recycling wastewater, both of which consume substantial amounts of energy.

The current energy sources in the region are heavily dependent on crude oil. Israel, for example, consumes 2.5 million tons of oil and 2.3 million tons of oil-equivalent of coal for the generation of electricity. The annual production of electricity amounted to 20.9 billion kWh at an installed capacity of 5,835 MW in 1991 (State of Israel, 1992). Because of its level of development, Israel is investigating the option of replacing its steam power generating system with nuclear plants in stages by the 21st century. A significant deficit in peak power supply has been a long standing problem, while substantial off-peak electricity is being wasted (Fig. 5-1). Although international networking of the electric supply is being discussed between Egypt and other Arab states, no alternatives have been suggested other than building a new pumped-storage unit and/or gas turbine generating units.

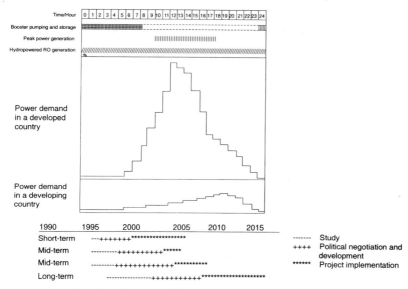

Fig. 5-1: Patterns of Daily Energy Generation and Use

A developed country's energy needs are closely related to its water supply. Substantial amounts of electricity can be consumed moving water from its sources to where it will be used. Pumping demand in Israel, for example, amounted to 1,528 KVA in 1991 (State of Israel, 1992), or 30 per cent of total expenditures on water supply by Mekorot, the national water development company. Israel, taking into account recent advances in desalination, is planning to introduce large-scale sea water desalination by the year 2000. Although this is likely to be dependent on low energy types of reverse osmosis, the energy cost will still be 50–60 per cent of the total depending on the price of electricity. Consequently the potential use of off-peak electricity will be a key element in minimizing the cost of water management and operation.

Techno-political Decision-making

Technical and policy water management options available to any watershed reaching the limits of its water supplies are listed in Table 5-1. Once the technical and policy options are known, the next, and probably the most crucial, step is to develop a method for evaluating the options against each other; that is, to create a hierarchy of viability. Many disciplines provide their own version of viability. Where an engineer might ask, 'Can it be done?' an economist might add, 'At what cost?' A political analyst could suggest, 'Is it politically feasible?' Anyone environmentally aware might counter, 'Should it be done at all?'

One problem with these varied standards of viability is that they often measure at cross-purposes, arriving at differing or even contradictory conclusions. Dinar and Wolf (1994), for example, have evaluated a potential Nile to Jordan basin water transfer, in terms of both economic and political viability. Their findings using each standard were diametrically opposite to each other: whereas an economic analysis suggested greater payoffs for co-operation between larger coalitions of states, a political investigation showed that the likelihood of such coalitions actually forming decreased as the size of the coalition increased, and that the most likely action was no co-operation whatsoever.

What we suggest here is a unified approach to overall viability which incorporates established measures for technical, environmental, economic, and political feasibility. Technical feasibility measures the physical parameters of a system or proposal—how much water might be produced? what is the quality? how reliable is the source? These physical parameters have well-defined quantitative values which might be used as indicators of viability. Quantity might be measured as volume of water produced by a project within a year. Likewise, quality might be evaluated in parts per million of total salinity or particular pollutants. A value for flux in a natural system or down-time in a technological project might be an indicator for reliability. On the other hand, control of flow variance (seasonal, multi-annual) can be counted as a positive factor. Relative environmental degradation can also be evaluated quantitatively, if impact assessments are performed uniformly between projects.

Economic viability has two aspects—financial, which measures the chances of acquiring financing for a project (often, but not always related to the amount of capital required), and efficiency. For relative water projects, one might use the results of a benefit/cost analysis and use the resulting net present value of benefits as a measure or, more directly, the cost per unit water which would result from each project. An important economic point is that costs are not fixed over time. A 'resource depletion curve' for any project would show at what rate the utility, or value, of a unit of water would begin to drop, and consequently, what the most efficient rate of development would be.

Table 5-1: WATER MANAGEMENT OPTIONS TO INCREASE
SUPPLY OR DECREASE DEMAND

Unilateral Options
Demand

- Population control
- Rationing
- Public awareness
- Allow price of water to reflect true costs (including national water market)
- Efficient agriculture, including:
- Drip irrigation
- Greenhouse technology
- Genetic engineering for drought and salinity resistance

Supply

- Wastewater reclamation
- Increase catchment and storage (including artificial groundwater recharge)
- Cloud seeding
- Desalination
- Fossil aquifer development

Co-operative Options

- Shared information and technology
- International water markets to increase distributive efficiency
- Inter-basin water transfers
- Joint regional planning

The most tenuous measure is political feasibility. To incorporate this important parameter in an integrated model, one must use a relative scale for a value which is difficult to quantify. While we recognize the general lack of enthusiasm for quantitative political analysis because of its necessarily subjective nature (Ascher, 1989, for a good critique), we recommend the inclusion of results of a process such as the PRINCE Political Accounting System. Coplin and O'-Leary (1976) describe this method of incorporating each player's 'position', 'power', and 'salience', for any of a number of policy options to arrive at a relative ranking of political viability. They extended the process to provide an absolute measure of the likelihood of a policy action taking place (Coplin and O'Leary, 1983).

Two other qualitative measures might be used for political

feasibility. For projects within a country, how well a proposal 'fits' with national goals might be evaluated. Population control, for example, which might be successful in western Europe or the United States, runs counter to both Israeli and Palestinian interests in numerical superiority. (Though even here at some not too distant time, population growth will impose an absolute ceiling on water availability). International projects might be determined in terms of relative measures for 'equity' of project costs and water distribution, and 'control' by each political entity of its own major water sources.

If the resources are available to perform a detailed feasibility study, the results can be described quantitatively. Listed below are the proposed measures of viability, followed by the possible quantitative standards which might be used (Table 5-2).

More often than not, the detailed data necessary for a quantitative evaluation are not available. In that case, two options exist. The first is to substitute qualitative values: +, 0, −, representing good, neutral, or poor; measures which are adequate for a preliminary analysis. We can then evaluate any possible option qualitatively with each measure of feasibility. This approach is illustrated in Table 5-3. By examining the results, we should get a sense of which options are more viable than others, and why. It should be remembered that these results are for a particular geographic location, and for a single point in time.

Table 5-3: POSSIBLE QUALITATIVE STANDARDS OF PROPOSED PROJECT VIABILITY MEASURES

Environmental
  • quantity (10^6 m^3/yr)
  • quality (ppm salinity or pollutants)
  • reliability of source (standard deviation of flux)
  • environmental impacts (details of potential damage)
Engineering
  • suitabiity of site
  • applicability and comparative outputs of various technologies
Economic
  • efficiency (cost per unit of water, or net present value of)
  • financial (capital necessary to finance project)
Political
  • political probability from PRINCE model
  • water distribution and control of source by each entity
  • equity of project costs

Table 5-2: TECHNO-POLITICAL ASSESSMENT SHEET—AS OF JULY 1994

Techno-Political Alternatives	Technical feasibility				Environmental feasibility	Economic feasibility			Political feasibility	Total
	Quantity	Quality	Reliability	Sub-total		Financial viability	Cost/unit water	Sub-total		
Weight (%)	12.5%	5.0%	7.5%	25.0%	25.0%	12.5%	12.5%	25.0%	25.0%	
Category 1: Water conservation, including supply and demand management										
Population control	74.0	80.0	98.0	82.4	65.0	72.0	86.0	79.0	10.0	59.1
Irrigation sector	80.0	84.0	84.0	82.0	69.0	68.0	70.0	69.0	39.0	67.3
M & I sector	54.0	63.0	84.0	64.8	84.0	69.0	62.0	65.5	33.0	61.8
Market solutions	60.0	75.0	70.0	66.0	66.3	80.0	77.5	78.8	41.3	63.1
Category 2: Conventional alternatives without political constraints										
Renewable surface water development	26.0	58.0	50.0	39.6	48.4	54.0	62.0	58.0	60.8	51.7
Renewable groundwater development	27.0	50.0	52.0	40.2	46.4	60.0	58.0	59.0	72.8	54.6
Category 3: Non-conventional alternatives without political constraints Desalination										
- Brackish groundwater RO desalination in M & I sector	52.5	83.8	80.8	67.2	61.3	77.5	75.0	76.3	66.8	67.9

(Contd.)

(Table 5-2 Contd.)

Techno-Political Alternatives	Technical feasibility				Environmental feasibility	Economic feasibility			Political feasibility	Total
	Quantity	Quality	Reliability	Sub-total		Financial viability	Cost/unit water	Sub-total		
Weight (%)	12.5%	5.0%	7.5%	25.0%	25.0%	12.5%	12.5%	25.0%	25.0%	
- Seawater RO and/or MSF de-salination in M & I sector	36.3	82.5	77.5	57.9	52.5	45.0	31.3	37.7	62.8	56.4
- RO desalination of brackish water: Peace Drainage Canal Project	31.0	66.0	62.0	47.3	55.8	61.0	61.0	61.0	69.0	58.3
Reuse and/or recycling treated wastewater										
- Reuse of treated urban wastewater for tree-crop irrigation	32.5	41.3	68.8	45.1	36.5	61.3	58.8	60.0	63.8	57.7
- Small scale recycling of treated industrial wastewater	36.3	66.3	72.5	45.2	60.3	60.0	45.0	52.5	57.5	55.4
Retention of *wadi* flash water										
- Small scale storage dam schemes for any use	27.5	65.0	52.5	42.5	48.0	47.0	43.8	45.4	62.3	49.5
- Small scale groundwater recharge scheme	25.0	66.3	65.0	45.3	46.8	60.0	57.5	58.8	62.3	53.3

(Contd.)

(Table 5-2 Contd.)

Techno-Political Alternatives	Technical feasibility				Environmental feasibility	Economic feasibility			Political feasibility	Total
	Quantity	Quality	Reliability	Sub-total		Financial viability	Cost/unit water	Sub-total		
Weight (%)	12.5%	5.0%	7.5%	25.0%	25.0%	12.5%	12.5%	25.0%	25.0%	
Category 4: Hydro-power/Storage										
Mini hydro-power (river development in Yarmuk)	31.5	60.0	47.5	42.0	40.0	31.7	40.0	35.8	38.5	39.1
Dead sea pumped storage	15.0	30.0	60.0	31.5	40.0	53.3	40.0	46.7	46.7	41.2
Mediterranean-Dead sea canal, without desalination	23.8	31.3	61.3	36.5	22.5	36.3	30.0	33.2	38.5	36.4
Red-Dead sea canal with/without solar pond for electricity development	21.3	30.0	28.8	25.3	22.5	33.8	30.0	31.9	31.0	27.7
Category 5: Co-generation alternative for water and energy										
MDS hydro-solar development with RO seawater desalination	40.0	72.5	60.0	52.5	45.0	33.8	33.8	33.8	35.3	41.7
Aqaba pumped-storage scheme with RO seawater de-salination	32.5	68.8	57.5	47.3	26.3	37.0	37.5	37.3	24.0	33.7
Red-Dead canal with solar pond/distilling de-salination (future tech.)	18.3	66.7	38.3	34.0	28.3	36.7	40.0	38.3	28.7	32.3

(Contd.)

(*Table 5-2 Contd.*)

Techno-Political Alternatives	Technical feasibility				Environmental feasibility	Economic feasibility			Political feasibility	Total
	Quantity	Quality	Reliability	Sub-total		Financial viability	Cost/unit water	Sub-total		
Weight (%)	12.5%	5.0%	7.5%	25.0%	25.0%	12.5%	12.5%	25.0%	25.0%	
Nuclear steam power plant with distilling seawater desalination	13.3	65.0	28.3	28.2	3.0	37.5	25.0	31.3	21.7	21.0
Category 6: Water transfer project by tankers or bags										
Inter-state water transfer by tankers	33.0	75.0	55.0	48.0	64.0	53.0	50.0	51.5	75.8	59.8
Inter-state water transfer by bags (Medusa concept)	31.0	79.0	45.0	44.8	52.0	46.0	48.0	47.0	68.3	53.0
Inter-state water transfer by bags (Aquarius concept)	25.0	81.7	58.3	46.3	53.3	46.7	56.7	51.7'	54.3	51.4
Category 7: Multi-lateral water transfer										
Nile-Gaza/Israel water pipeline	49.0	64.0	51.0	52.6	33.0	48.0	54.0	51.0	7.0	35.9
Iraq-Jordan water pipeline	36.0	47.0	27.0	35.5	30.2	44.0	54.0	49.0	10.4	31.3
Litani (Lebanon-Jordan) basin water transfer	38.4	67.0	51.0	47.9	43.2	56.0	59.0	57.5	9.6	39.6
Mini-mini-peace pipeline (Turkey-Syria)	31.3	55.0	53.8	42.8	34.0	45.0	61.0	53.0	23.8	38.4

(*Contd.*)

(*Table 5-2 Contd.*)

Techno-Political Alternatives	Technical feasibility				Environmental feasibility	Economic feasibility			Political feasibility	Total
	Quantity	Quality	Reliability	Sub-total		Financial viability	Cost/unit water	Sub-total		
Weight (%)	12.5%	5.0%	7.5%	25.0%	25.0%	12.5%	12.5%	25.0%	25.0%	
Mini-pipeline (Turkey-Syria-Jordan river basin, pipeline)	32.5	56.3	55.0	44.0	36.5	45.0	50.0	47.5	23.3	37.8
Mini-pipeline (Syria, Euphrates-Jordan basins)	32.5	57.5	65.0	47.3	34.0	45.0	50.0	47.5	23.3	38.0
Peace pipeline (Turkey-Persian Gulf, Red sea)	48.0	54.0	36.0	45.6	30.8	28.0	28.0	28.0	8.2	28.2
Peace canal (Turkey-Syria-Jordan River Basin, incl. security barrier)	32.5	47.5	37.5	37.0	18.0	27.5	31.3	29.4	5.5	22.5
Turkey-Israel submarine water pipeline	32.0	52.0	21.2	32.8	32.8	23.0	23.0	23.0	13.4	25.5
Mega watershed (Rift Valley groundwater development)	28.8	13.8	10.0	20.1	7.3	13.8	13.8	13.8	6.3	11.8

Note: Without 26 Oct. 1994 Treaty of Peace: Israel/Jordan. *See* Table 6-4, Chapter 6, for post-Treaty Evaluation.

Although the 'Total' column is provided for a measure of overall feasibility, it is recommended that, if the column is used at all, it is used with extreme caution. First, each measure does not necessarily have equal weight, and each was arrived at with both some subjectivity and some uncertainty. Adding or multiplying across would therefore only compound and accumulate error.

Also, by leaving the measures separate, one acquires a greater sense of why options are viable, and where emphasis can be placed for the future in order to help boost viability. Public awareness, for example, has been shown to be a very cost-effective method of saving water, but the total amount which can be saved is relatively small as compared to the total water budget. In contrast, unlimited water can be made available through desalination but at a relatively higher cost. The latter might change with technologic breakthroughs, but conservation gains are likely to remain fairly constant over time.

The second option in the absence of data necessary for a quantitative assessment is to substitute iterations of 'expert opinions', first described by Gordon and Helmer (1964) as the Delphi method.[3] Experts familiar with the technical and political landscapes of a particular watershed might be asked to rank available options as to their viabilities on a consistent scale. The viability measures themselves should also be weighted as to their relative importance for that particular watershed during a particular time frame. A variation on the weighting process is first described in detail in Kepner and Tregoe (1965).

It should be emphasized that this evaluation process should be repeated often to allow for the constant changes of so many of the parameters over space and time.

The evaluation process should also allow for interaction, with on-going feedback between the disciplines, to reflect real-world influences. For example, a project with extremely positive economic results might help overcome political reluctance to enter into cooperation. Likewise, political constraints can effectively veto a project which has been judged worthwhile in terms of its technical and economic value. Changes which can affect viability are shown in Table 5-4.

Table 5-4: CHANGES AFFECTING PROJECT VIABILITY

Technical and Environmental

- Fluctuations in seasonal and annual water supply, as well as long-term changes due to global warming
- Changes in water quality
- Technical breakthroughs
- Relative infrastructure for each party in
  research and development
  storage and delivery
- Changes in understanding of physical system

Economic

- Changing priorities for funding agencies
- Movement along the resource depletion curve
- Expense for water resources development
- Changes in efficiency of water use

Political

- Power relationships
  riparian position
  military
  legal (e.g., clarity of water rights)
- Form and stability of government
- Level of hostility

SPECIFIC OPTIONS AND TECHNO-POLITICAL FEASIBILITIES

Perspectives of Non-conventional Water Development Alternatives

Conventional alternatives, which include surface water and ground water development, have the highest priority in water resources planning where there are still renewable fresh waters to be developed and intricate inter-state riparian questions do not result. This ideal situation does not exist in most countries of the Middle East, and the supplying of fresh potable water to their growing populations is an essential part of a water master plan for peace. Every possible source of water must be seriously considered, and water conservation is and will be an essential part of water management. After exploiting all of the renewable fresh water resources within their national boundaries, Israel, Palestine, and Jordan will have no choice except to seek extra-territorial sources of supply and/or non-conventional waters. Surplus waters from the periphery might be provided by means of long distance pipelines and/or tankers and sea borne bags, but these alternatives should not be brought on line until sources within the basin are being used at their most efficient. Therefore, development of non-conventional water alternatives is becoming imperative. A general list of water development priorities is shown in Table 5-5.

Non-conventional alternatives, which comprise desalination, and reuse of treated wastewater will be key issues to sustain water development into the 21st century, when no additional, renewable fresh water will be available. Fossil groundwater by contrast is usually too valuable an asset except as a strategic reserve which can be used for short-term relief during extreme drought or emergencies. The general characteristics of non-conventional water resources will be that they are generally more complex in development and operation than conventional sources, and are almost always more expensive. The great advantage of desalination and reuse of treated waste water is that there are few political constraints to their development. The unlimited supply of sea water is another advantage for desalination, especially since 70 per cent of the Arab and Israeli populations live near and along the sea coast. This situation favours Israel and the Gaza Strip; less so Jordan, which has sea access only at Aqaba; and is not helpful to the West Bank, which has no sea access.

Table 5-5: TECHNICAL-POLITICAL PRIORITIES: LOWER JORDAN
SYSTEM AND DEAD SEA

Israel

Water conservation, improving existing infrastructure and delivery systems

Desalination including both brackish water and sea water

Reuse of treated wastewater for tree and/or garden crop irrigation

Retention of wadi flush water including groundwater recharge

Mediterranean-Dead sea (MDS) conduit scheme for cogeneration

Water management of the Jordan valley including desalination of brackish springs and waste saline water from drainage network, perhaps in conjunction with the West Bank and/or Jordan

Dead sea pumped-storage for peak-power supply

Inter-state water transfer and importation by tankers or bags including pipeline options from Nile and Turkey

Dead sea solar-pond scheme and/or Aqaba ocean heat-energy conversion scheme (future technology)

Palestine (West Bank)

Water conservation, improving existing infrastructure and delivery systems

Groundwater management of mountain aquifer

Retention of wadi flush water including groundwater recharge

Sanitation of wastewater including reuse for tree and/or garden crop irrigation

Water management of the Jordan valley including desalination of brackish springs and waste saline water from drainage network, perhaps with Israel and/or Jordan

Inter-state water transfer such as mini-peace pipeline from Turkey

Palestine (Gaza)

Water conservation, improving existing infrastructure and delivery systems

Groundwater management of coastal aquifer

Retention of flush water including groundwater recharge

Sanitation of wastewater including reuse for crop irrigation

Desalination of brackish groundwater and sea water

Inter-state water transfer and importation by tankers or bags, including water pipeline option from Nile

Jordan

Water conservation, improving existing infrastructure and delivery systems

Conventional unilateral river development including storage dams on the *Wadi* Mujib, Wadi Hasa and other small tributaries

Inter-state river development including storage dam on the Yarmouk (Al-Wuheda dam), taking into account the coupling of the MDS canal project.

Retention of wadi flush water including groundwater recharge

Sanitation of wastewater including reuse for tree and/or garden crop irrigation

Water resources management of fossil groundwater in Disi sandstone aquifer

Water management of the Azraq and Jordan valley including desalination of brackish springs and waste saline water from drainage network; perhaps with Israel and/or the West Bank (Palestine) in the Jordan Valley

Desalination of brackish water in Azraq, Jordan Valley including Aqaba-Disi hydro-powered brackish groundwater reverse osmosis desalination for co-generation (Murakami 1991)

Desalination of sea water in Aqaba region including hybrid pumped-storage scheme with hydro-powered reverse osmosis desalination

Red-Dead sea canal hydro-electric scheme or Dead sea pumped-storage scheme for peak-power supply

Dead sea solar-pond scheme and/or Aqaba (deep sea water) ocean heat-energy conversion scheme (future technology)

After renewable water resources have been utilized to the limits of sustainable yield, new strategies will become increasingly important: 1) water conservation will be essential to maintain and extend water yields; and 2) water politics and negotiations will be priority issues in any trans-boundary water development project. In addition, 3) environmentally sound, innovative, technological development with reasonable cost reduction will be a key issue in non-conventional water development, as defined below. A number of such projects have been suggested for application in the core area. A general description of them follows.

DESCRIPTION OF POSSIBLE PROJECTS

The schemes referred to above include, in order of conceptualizaton:
1. Mediterranean to Dead sea (Med-Dead) canal, or
2. Red sea to Dead sea (Red-Dead) canal,
3. Pumped storage, including locations at a) Aqaba, b) on the eastern and western shores of the Dead sea, and c) on the eastern shore of the sea of Galilee,
4. Jordan valley drainage canal, and
5. Desalination.

Med–Dead canal

The height differential between the Mediterranean sea, at sea level, and the Dead sea, 400 metres lower, suggests the possibility of linking the two water bodies to generate hydro-power. Such plans date back to the last century, but were studied seriously in the late 1970's, as rising oil costs encouraged Israel to investigate alternative energy sources. Initially, feasibility studies investigated three northern routes, eventually considered less viable for economic and environmental reasons, and a southern route, from Qatif in the Gaza strip through the Judean hills, to Massada on the south-western shore of the Dead sea. This last route has received maximum attention. Although plans were shelved in the 1980s as energy costs dropped, the project has recently been revived in the Israel-Palestine Declaration of Principles.

Pumping and power generation would proceed at two different levels: during a filling period of twenty years the Dead sea would be brought back to its historic water level. This would involve pumping

1,670 mcm/yr and would generate an average of 1,850 GWh/yr. Thereafter, 1,250 mcm/yr would be pumped, just matching the evaporation rate of the Dead sea, which would generate 1,450 GWh/yr. Several ancillary projects based on a supply of salt-water in the heart of the Negev desert have been proposed in conjunction with the canal project. These might allow for aquaculture, tourism along artificial lakes, and cooling water for industry. Most salient for this study, though, is the fact that the 400 metre drop to the Dead sea would provide the pressure necessary for reverse osmosis desalination, as will be explored later in this text.

Red–Dead canal

Similar in concept to the Med-Dead canal, the Red-Dead canal would exploit the 400 metre height differential between the Red sea and the Dead sea for hydro-power generation. The project was studied intensely in the late 1970's as Jordan's answer to Israel's Med-Dead studies, and has recently been mentioned as a possible joint project in the Israel-Jordan peace treaty. It should be noted that, because pumping rates must eventually match the Dead sea's evaporation rates, it would not be feasible to construct both canal projects.

The Red-Dead canal, as described in a Jordanian feasibility study by Harza Engineering, was designed as a peaking facility to operate eight hours per day, and would generate an average of 975 GWh/yr. As with the Med-Dead canal, a canal linking the Red and Dead seas would be conducive to ancillary projects, including aquaculture, tourism, and industry. Planners also discussed a desalination component although, because the hydro-power would be generated in a series of steps to the Dead sea, the loss of head may render reverse osmosis desalination uneconomical.

Pumped Storage

Just as height differentials can be exploited to generate hydro-power, they can also provide sites for pumped storage. Pumped storage is a method to meet peak energy demand by pumping from a lower water body when power needs and costs are low to a reservoir at a higher elevation. When energy demand and costs are at their peak, the water is dropped back down to the original water body, generating hydro-power in the process. While no new energy is generated, pumped storage helps smooth energy demand, alleviating the need to build more power-generating facilities. Good pumped storage sites have been identified throughout the core region, including one at Aqaba, two sites on the east and west coast of the Dead sea, and another on the eastern shore of the Sea of Galilee. It should be noted that pumped storage facilities do not, in themselves, provide new sources of water, but can provide energy and/or pressure for desalination.

Jordan Valley Salt/Peace Drainage canal

Agriculture in the core region accounts for more than 75 per cent of the total water demand. However, not all water applied to irrigation is consumed by evapotranspiration. Water which infiltrates past the root zone, referred to as agricultural drainage water, or return flow (RF), can sometimes be reclaimed. The problem with this water is that its quality is relatively poor, as it can include salts, pesticides, and herbicides.

Nevertheless, in regions where desalination is viable, the lower the salinity, the less expensive the desalting process. This RF is relatively less saline than other sources, with average total dissolved solids of 1,000–10,000 ppm, as compared with 33,000 ppm for sea water. (Drinking water generally requires less than 500 ppm.) Drainage projects can be implemented on both slopes of the Jordan river valley, allowing for relatively inexpensive desalination. These might also desalinize water from salt springs which at the present time further pollute the lower stem of the Jordan river.

Desalination

Oceans are the ultimate source and destination of all of the world's freshwater. As such, they offer a relatively unlimited supply of water for human uses, limited only by economical technology and potential environmental impact. Current research generally focuses on two methods to desalinize water:

1) *Flash distillation.* When water boils, only pure water turns to steam—the salts which are in solution remain behind in an increasingly saline brine. Flash distillation plants generally include a series of chambers ('multi-stage flash') at progressively lower pressures. Salt

water brought through the chambers flashes into vapour at lower temperatures in each chamber, resulting in extremely pure water. Flash distillation plants are more common where thermal, as against electrical, energy is available, and where seawater, rather than brackish water, is the source to be desalinized. Because this method best uses thermal energy, a common practice to reduce costs is to site distillation desalination projects next to traditional energy-generating plants. This takes advantage of the waste heat or excess power generated. Flash distillation currently accounts for 65 per cent of the world's desalination plants.

2) *Reverse osmosis.* This method of desalination involves pushing saline water at high pressures through selective membranes, which are designed to remove salts. This method more commonly uses electric energy, therefore allowing RO plants to be situated independent of power generating facilities. Such plants more commonly desalinize brackish water. Because this process requires mechanical pressure, costs for reverse osmosis desalination can be reduced when a large elevation drop exists along the water delivery system, as for example, along the Med-Dead or Red-Dead canal routes. Reverse osmosis desalination currently accounts for 23 per cent of the world's desalination plants.

Two problems limit desalination: economy and environment. Although drinking water is a completely inelastic good—that is, people will pay almost any price for it—water for agriculture, by far the largest use in the Middle East, should be cost-effective enough that the agricultural end-product remains competitive in the marketplace. Current cost estimates for desalination, approximately $1.60 to $2.70 per cubic meter to de-salt sea water, and from 30 to 50 cents for brackish water, leave desalinated water uneconomic for most uses. It also should be kept in mind that price estimates generally do not include pumping costs of getting the water to the end-users. Most sources for desalination are at sea level and along coasts, while consumers are more often at higher elevations and further inland. Therefore, the use of desalinized sea water is limited to the coastal area.

TECHNO-POLITICAL ALTERNATIVES IN ISRAEL, PALESTINE, AND JORDAN

The priorities for techno-political alternatives as assessed in the evaluation framework differ in each state depending on the development level of water resources. Techno-political priorities for the major riparians of the lower Jordan system and Dead sea are shown in Table 5-5.

Techno-political feasibility for specific projects within a watershed can be evaluated quantitatively, as described above. In our case the specific techno-political options available to the riparians of the Jordan river watershed are evaluated qualitatively, since the information necessary for most of these projects is not available, and can only be arrived at through detailed feasibility studies. These are transferred, following the PRINCE technique, into a feasability table (Table 6.3). Each option is listed in the first column of Table 6.3, followed by columns for the four measures of feasibility—technical (sub-divided into quantity, quality, and reliability), environmental, Economic (sub-divided into financial viability, and cost per unit water), and political.

Derivation of Percentage Values and 'Multiplying Across'

Overall feasibility for each project on the 'Techno-Political Assessment Sheet' is considered to be a function of four parameters — technical, environmental, economic, and political feasibility. Since each parameter is considered equally, each score (determined through 'Delphi' style discussions, on a scale of 0–100) is weighed by 25 per cent. For the first 'project' considered, 'Population Control', for example, the total feasibility measure, 59.1 was derived by adding each feasibility sub-total weighted by 25 per cent.

$(82.5 \times 25$ per cent$) + (65.0 \times 25$ per cent$) = (79.0 \times 25$ per cent$) + (10.0 \times 25$ per cent$) = 59.1$

Each feasibility sub-total, in turn, was derived by adding the components which make up each parameter, also weighed by the value given on the top line. The technical feasibility sub-total for 'Population control' of 82.4, was derived as follows:

([Quantity] $74.0 \times$ [Weight] 12.5 per cent) + ([Quantity] $80 \times$ [Weight] 5.0 per cent) + ([Reliability] $98.0 \times$ [Weight] 7.5 per cent) $\times 4 = 82.4$

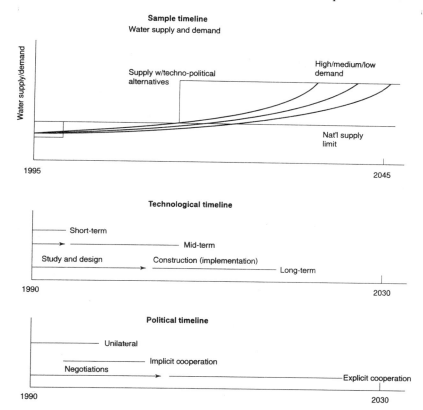

Fig. 5-2: Water Availability, Technological and Political Timelines

Each project is then evaluated for each measure, which in turn is given a relative weight, after Kepner and Tregoe (1965). The values reported were derived through a modified Delphi process, averaging subjective values assigned by the members of the Middle East Water Commission at a meeting in June, 1994. Multiplying across gives us a total value for the overall feasibility of each project.[4] Again, it should be remembered that these values are assigned for a particular geographical location for one specific point in time. This process should ideally be iterative to allow for changes in the system and interaction between the different aspects of viability.

In general, the relatively higher rankings of unilateral options indicate greater chances of succes, but the smaller values associated with them, which signify less water, suggest that while there is still some hydrologic room to manoeuvre within each political entity, such options are limited. Conversely, if co-operative measures become politically feasible, the quantities of water which could be made available are significant. This suggests, that the hypothetical rewards of co-operation might be used as incentives at the negotiating table.

In addition, time is a major variable in prioritizing specific projects within a basin. While negotiating, water rights and allocation may take years to resolve, in the meantime, some immediate steps can be implemented. Likewise, while most water managers agree that mega-projects involving inter-basin transfers or large-scale desalination may be best suited for the future, planning and evaluating such projects needs to be done immediately in order for the resulting water to arrive at results to be used 10 or 15 years from now.

Project priorities among the technical-political alternatives are evaluated by taking into account the projects' time schedules. These are illustrated in Figure 5-2.

TECHNO-POLITICAL OPTIONS

The evaluation framework, combined with chronological considerations, suggests the following schedule and planning timeline for water resources development within the Jordan river watershed (Fig. 5-3).

```
1990      1995      2000       2005     2010     2015
Short-term    ---+++++++*******************
Mid-term (1)  ----------+++++++++++++++
Mid-term (2)  ----------+++++++++++++++++***********
Long-term     -------------------+++++++++++**********************
```

```
-------   Study, political negotiation and development,
++++      Project implementation,
******    Supplemental implementation.
```

Fig. 5-3: Scheduling Timelines for Water Resources Development in the Jordan Valley

1.*Short-term relief*: highest priority and urgent needs in water development and management—no political constraints.

- Water conservation and water demand management
-Reuse of treated wastewater (for supplemental tree-crop irrigation)
-Desalination (for potable water supply mainly by reverse osmosis)

2. *Mid-term relief* (1): high priority in the water-energy development plans included in strategic peace agreements between Israel, Palestine, and Jordan. These in turn may reinforce ongoing peace negotiations, with benefits for multilateral regional economic development opportunities in the Dead sea and Aqaba region:

Priority
1. The Lower Jordan Salt/Peace Drainage canal scheme with brackish water desalination
2. Mediterranean (Gaza) -Dead sea (MDS) conduit scheme with hydro-powered RO desalination for co-generation
3. Aqaba sea water pumped-storage scheme with hydro-powered RO desalination for co-generation
4. Red-Dead sea (RDS) or MDS canal hydro-electric scheme
5. Dead sea pumped-storage scheme

3. *Mid-term relief* (2): medium priority in the water supply alternatives with some bilateral negotiations with water rich countries such as Turkey, Albania, Greece, and south Asian countries:
-Interstate water transportation by tankers and/or bags

4. *Long-term relief:* medium to low priority (though no less important) with complicated multinational riparian negotiations and/or technical-economical-financial elements. These will be evaluated in Chapter Seven.
-Interstate water transportation by pipeline, canal, and others are illustrated in key map (2), including
-Nile-Gaza/Israel water pipeline,
-Iraq-Jordan water pipeline,
-Litani-Jordan basin (Lebanon-Israel) water transfer,
-Mini-peace pipeline (Seyhan-Ceyhan-Jordan river system),
-Turkish (Ozal's) Peace pipeline,
-Peace canal (Golan heights),
- Medusa bags (seaborne), and
-Trans-Syrian pipeline (Lake Assad to Yarmouk headwaters).

CONCLUSIONS

The inter-disciplinary needs of water resources planning draw the hydrologist, engineer, economist, and political analyst increasingly closer, and each will have to learn a necessary portion of the others' languages. Hydrologic variations in water supply and demand, political considerations of equity, control, and ideology, and economic measures of marginal utility and comparative advantage, all interact to determine overall feasibility of solutions to international water issues.

The international supplying and delivery of water is becoming increasingly more feasible with the growth of water deficits at the core. As this occurs, the political aspects of particular basins will take on greater importance in the process of water resources decision-making and planning. Too often, technological and political considerations both within and outside a given watershed are treated separately, inconsistently, and with little regard for each other. The process for incorporating both aspects in a unified 'techno-political' evaluation framework, as described here, may facilitate the beginnings of truly integrated planning.

NOTES

1. For more in-depth discussions of both the hydro-political positions and the technical and policy options available to the riparians of the Jordan basin, the reader is referred to Murakami (1994) and Wolf (1994).

2. As with all such figures, exact data and agreement among data sets is difficult or impossible to achieve. Lonergan and Brooks (Table 7, p. 72) show the following values: Domestic Water–Litres PC/day: Israel within Green Line = 125; West Bank: Israeli Settlements = 250; Palestinian Villages = 40; Towns = 100; Gaza Strip = 85.

3. *See* Linstone and Turoff (1975) for a good summary of the strengths, weaknesses, and applications of the Delphi method: Needham and de Loë (1990) for its applicability to water resources planning.

4. We recognize the extreme subjectivity of the outcome of this excercise, as necessitated by limited information. Nevertheless, we feel that the process described, however, provides a useful tool for systematic decision-making, incorporating the technical and political concerns of development inherent in any watershed.

6 Techno-Political Water and Energy Development Alternatives from the Mediterranean and Red Seas to the Jordan Rift Valley

INTRODUCTION

Owing to the unique geo-political character of the Dead sea and its valley, joint regional development planning received a prominent place in the September 1993 Agreement of Principles between Israel and the PLO (Israel/PLO, 1993). Regional economic development being conceived as a key element to sustain the peace process in the region, the protocol on Israel-PLO relations suggests that priority be given to certain projects including development of the Dead sea region and the Red sea (Aqaba)—Dead sea pipeline (RSDS) (Fig. 6-1). The weak point of the bilateral agreement was that it did not at that stage include the kingdom of Jordan as a major riparian state on the Dead sea and Jordan river. On 26 October 1994 this situation was rectified in part by the signing of a peace treaty between Jordan and Israel. Palestine, however, remained an outsider to those negotiations, and the need for a tripartite agreement continues.

As post-treaty details continue to be worked out, the Aqaba region will become even more important for water and power development both in the short-and the long-term. In addition, the Aqaba bay area has great potential for the development of international tourism, commerce and industry.[1] Owing to its hyper-arid climate, however, limited water supplies, exacerbated by political difficulties, have been the main constraint to development.

This study suggests a unified approach to regional water planning including two additional core projects for regional co-operation through the co-generation of water and electric power: the Mediter-ranean-Dead sea conduit scheme (MDS)[2] and the Aqaba sea water

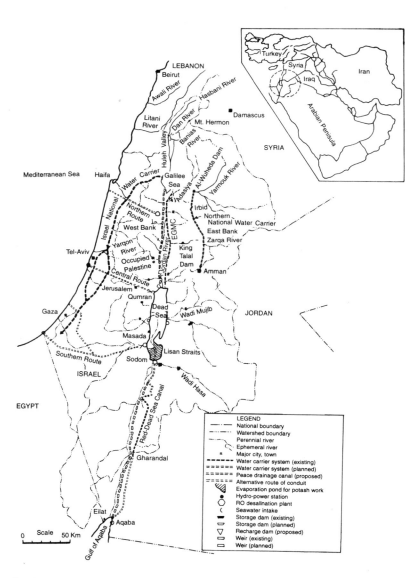

Fig. 6-1: Water Resources Development Project Alternatives in the Jordan River System

pumped-storage scheme (Fig. 6-1). These would take into account the following possible scenarios for sharing resources and benefits:

1) An interstate electricity grid or network including Egypt, Israel, Palestine, Jordan, Saudi Arabia, and perhaps Syria and Lebanon, to provide cheap off-peak electricity to pumped-storage schemes, could be incorporated in the Aqaba and RSDS and or MDS plan to provide peak energy and balance the grid.

2) Techno-political priority in the Dead sea region development portion of the inter-state regional development plan might be given to (a) an MDS conduit cogenerating scheme, and (b) an Aqaba hybrid pumped-storage co-generation scheme.

3) An inter-state coastal water pipeline, to connect the three states (Jordan, Israel, Egypt) , to share fresh potable water from a hydro-powered reverse osmosis desalination plant proposed for the Aqaba co-generating pumped-storage scheme.

4) An interstate sanitation and environmental management programme including wastewater recovery for tree crop irrigation and protection of the clean water environment of Aqaba bay.[3]

In a broader context, the Aqaba sea water pumped storage plan— with hydro-powered reverse osmosis (RO) desalination—is possibly of greatest importance for the economic development of the region. Such a scheme would be highly competitive when compared with a single purpose hydro-power scheme such as Dead sea pumped-storage or a Med/Dead or Red/Dead sea canal.

The funding for such schemes may be forthcoming. Even without an anticipated 'Marshal' type plan for a Mideast at peace, one might assume a certain 'peace dividend' for countries no longer locked in a regional arms race. This dividend might be re-allocated to peaceful development. Water resource improvement is high on the list of developmental priorities for all parties in the region, particularly in light of both imminent and on going influxes of immigrants and refugees. The pooling of investment resources and planning would allow for greater flexibility in design and, consequently, would lead to greater economic efficiency.

In view of such possibilities, it is necessary to review the water/energy development alternatives in the two inter-state regions of the Dead sea and Aqaba as shown in Table 5.4. This should be done in the context of sharing resources and benefits, meanwhile taking into account the next possible multilateral peace agreement among Israel, Palestine represented by the PLO and Jordan. It should also be remembered that the riparian states of Syria and Lebanon as well as neighbouring Egypt and Saudi Arabia could share resources and benefits resulting from such a peace arrangement.

After this review of local projects of possible benefit to the regional core, Chapter 7 examines the augmentation of core water supplies with additions from the periphery.

HISTORICAL BACKGROUND: NUCLEAR DESALINATION AND MED/DEAD SEA CANAL PROJECTS

Immediately after the Six-Day War in 1967, former US President Dwight D Eisenhower, Lewis Strauss of the Atomic Energy Commission, and Alvin Weinberg, Director of the Oak Ridge National Laboratories, developed a 'water for peace' project on a massive scale for the Mideast. It included a series of nuclear desalination plants that would have provided power and water for immense 'agro-industrial' complexes which, it was hoped, would have eased political tensions caused by refugees and water scarcity (Oak Ridge National Laboratory, 1971).

The plan was given a boost by the US Senate Resolution 155 (Congressional Quarterly Almanac, 1967), which expressed support for development at three likely sites in Egypt, Israel, and Jordan. Recently de-classified reports show that a fourth site, at Gaza, was also planned in conjunction with a project for refugee resettlement. The plan eventually faltered on political and economic grounds. Nevertheless, two years of co-operative research between Americans, Arabs, and Israelis, along with lessons learnst during the Johnston negotiations twelve years earlier, showed that, on the technical level at least, cooperation over regional water resources and planning was possible.

However, the idea of introducing nuclear desalination plants was too optimistic to apply worldwide to every country. This resulted from a failure to reduce costs, as well as an increasing concern regarding the environmental impact of nuclear development. There was also a specific concern about introducing nuclear technology in the Middle East.

Today, improved sea water desalination technology including the reverse osmosis (RO) process suggests its marginal feasibility for supplying the municipal and industrial (M and I) sectors in arid regions. Nevertheless, RO is not economically feasible for use with extensive crop irrigation.

In the early 1980s, fifteen years after the American vetoing of nuclear desalination plants, the Israelis began planning a canal, designed primarily for hydro-power, to bring Mediterranean sea water across the Negev desert and under the Judean hills, in order to drop it 400 meters to the Dead sea, the lowest point on earth.

Study of the Mediterranean-Dead sea (MDS) canal emphasized five main alternative canal routes from a total of 27 considered: 1) a northern route, 2) a southern route a, 3) a southern route b , 4) a central route , and 5) the Aqaba/Dead sea route , as shown in Fig. 6-1. The minimum length route, i.e., the 'central route' canal, would have been 72 km long, including a 15 km section of open canal and a 57 km tunnel 5 m in diameter (WPDC, 1983). The first 30 km section would have crossed Israeli territory, and the second 42 km section would have traversed the West Bank. This option was, however, put-aside for fear of possible saline (sea water) water leakage from the tunnel into fresh groundwater aquifers underlying the Judean mountain range upon which Israel relies for 30 per cent of its water supply. The possibility of potential environmental degradation effectively ended an earlier proposal for a canal project through the Jezreel and Jordan valleys (Stern and Gradus). In final analysis the 'Gaza-Ein Bokek' route with an 80 km tunnel was selected in 1982 to minimize capital costs and environment impact. The selected route, however, would cross the occupied Gaza strip, as shown in Fig. 6-1. For political reasons, an alternative route was considered which would move the entrance of the canal northwards into Israeli territory. This would have added $60 million to the cost, and 20 km to the planned 100 km-length (WPDC, 1985). Even had political problems in the Gaza strip been avoided, they would certainly have arisen *vis-á-vis* Jordan, which shares the Dead sea with Israel.

The Israeli MDS solar-hydro development project (see below p. 107) would have generated 800 MW electricity with annual production of 1.4–1.85 × 10^9 kWh.[4] The official total project cost was estimated to be $1.89 billion (1990 prices). Later estimates ranged upward to $5 billion. The planned effect of the canal was to raise the level of the Dead sea by 17 m from 402 to 385 m below sea level. This would have meant that mineral processing plants in both countries would have had to be moved and potash production could have fallen by 15 per cent (WPDC, 1983). The value of the 800 megawatts (MW) installed capacity that would have been made available by this Med-Dead canal would have just equalled the cost of the project. Although the benefits of several ancillary projects for cooling or for artificial lakes made possible by the saltwater added viability to the scheme (Mediterranean-Dead sea Co., Ltd, 1983) the project was finally shelved due to the question of unfavourable project economies owing to the substantial decrease in the cost of crude oil after 1983.

Although an exciting project, the original Med-Dead canal focused on power generation rather than on water production. Moreover, it was unilateral in scope, bringing benefits only to Israel. In fact, Palestinians objected to the proposed site of the intake at Qatif, on the ground that it would further integrate Gaza with Israel. Jordan protested the anticipated rise in the level of the shared Dead sea. As a result, three separate resolutions condemning the proposal were brought before the United Nations General Assembly. Jordan took the opportunity, however, to investigate the possibility of a similar, but for the time even more short-lived, project of its own, the 'Red-Dead' canal, which is now being reconsidered.

The 'Red-Dead' canal would have been similar to the Med-Dead canal, with the major difference being the source of water for hydro-power—in this case the Red sea. The flow of water from the Jordanian carrier would have forced Israel to cut back its own influx of water into the Dead sea, or the level would have risen high enough to flood the potash works of both Israel and Jordan as well as the seaside hotels on the Israeli shore.

Israeli interest then turned to salt water pumped storage from the Dead sea (WPDC, 1989). It should be noted that a United Nations mission suggested that the maximum level to have been reached by the Dead sea would have been 390.5 m. Because this level was comparable with previous equilibrium levels, it would not have flooded any religious or archaeological sites, nor would it have triggered earthquakes, nor would reflectivity have been increased.

The Original Red-Dead Canal Scheme

The project was designed as a peaking facility, with sea water being pumped to an elevation of 215 m, and then put into a series of canals and reservoirs to Safe, 200 km farther north (Fig.1). The Red-Dead sea canal hydro-electric project would have generated 334 MW (975 GWh per annum) for 8 hours a day for peak power demand (WPDC, 1983). The booster pumping scheme included two pumping stations with an installed capacity of 70 MW and a required power output of 615 GWh per annum. The estimated total construction cost was about JD 453 million at the 1990 price ($ 680 million) (JVA, 1981).

NEW OPPORTUNITIES FOR REGIONAL DEVELOPMENT

Despite the failure of these previously suggested projects to be approved, the best aspects of the regional approach—i.e., the Med-Dead or Red-Dead canals, emphasis on international economic co-operation, and comparatively safe and clean energy applications—can still be combined and integrated with new co-generation technology for water and electricity. These could subsequently, by the year 2000, be expanded into a new hybrid project for water and power. The project, in turn, could be incorporated into a badly needed regional water development plan for the entire Middle East. It is this potential situation which is discussed in the pages that follow.

Conceptual Framework

The core of the complex might be either a Med-Dead or a Red-Dead canal with a new emphasis on reverse osmosis desalination fueled by direct hydro-pressure based on a topographic head difference of 400–600 m. In contrast to the earlier plans, which focused on unilateral power generation and development, a new approach would make available, in sparsely populated areas, power for industry and water for fish ponds and even recreation on artificial lakes. This would benefit people from Egypt, Israel, Jordan, and Palestine. The scope of the project could be expanded, depending upon cost, financing, and which of the countries and territories of the region become involved. Greater benefits would accrue with larger scale involvement.

Regardless of whether the Red-Dead or the Med-Dead scheme is or will be chosen, the focus on water, rather than power, and an emphasis on co-operative regional development instead of unilateral benefits, would add both the economic and the political feasibility that earlier plans have lacked.

The original Med-Dead saltwater canal would have been situated in a particularly opportune position to foster regional co-operation. A similar new project can do the same. The originally proposed intake was to be located in or near the Gaza strip, the site of the most densely populated refugee camps in the world, which suffers from a severe groundwater overdraft. The canal itself would have run parallel to the Egyptian-Israeli border and then through the Negev-Sinai deserts. The cogeneration canal project proposed here could do the same. Ancillary developments plus new supplies of power and water (both fresh and salt or brackish) would do much to alleviate the desperate human needs of this area.

The Med-Dead route or the Red-Dead route would each face obstacles in terms of political viability, as have all plans for regional co-operation. However, the Mediterranean (Gaza)-Dead sea canal has just been revived in the 'Declaration of Principles', 13 September 1993, in which Annex-IV: Protocol on Israeli-Palestinian Actions suggests a project based on the Med-Dead canal.

The 400-metre drop into the Dead sea valley could provide not only hydro-power generation, but also make reverse osmosis de-salination feasible. The hydro-pressure of $40-60 \text{ kg/cm}^2$ could be used directly to desalinize sea water by membrane permeation (RO) at a reasonable treatment cost of less than $1.00/\text{m}^3$.

Although a Red-Dead canal scheme would do much the same for Israel and Jordan, the topography and geology of the Red-Dead route are not favourable for combining hydro-power generation with a desalination plant in a single pressure pipe line system. Such a system, which would require a terminal end pressure at $40-60 \text{ kg/m}^2$ for RO, would necessitate initial pumping to a higher elevation—albeit off peak power would make this a relatively cheap operation. Thereafter, the distance and topographic profile from the Gulf of Aqaba to the Dead sea is relatively gradual and would necessitate a stepped descent. If open canals were included in the design, such stepping, would obviate the hydraulic head necessary for successful RO desalination in combination with hydro-power generation. A closed pipeline ensuring the necessary pressure would be more complicated and expensive to build. At the same time, much of the route crosses unstable lithology. The *Lisan Marl* thus involved is friable and easily dissolved, and at best would provide an unstable base for such construction, further exacerbated by the possibility of earthquakes in the Rift valley.

Conversely, the existing design of the Med-Dead (central) conduit route shows an ideal profile for placing a reverse osmosis desalination plant at the end of the pressure pipeline system, as well as a better lithologic configuration.

Other Options

Ideas exist for using sea water along the routes of either the Med-Dead or Red-Dead canals for the purpose of irrigation. Ample agricultural land is found along the routes, but these schemes will depend on the future development and progress in biotechnology for irrigating crops with sea water.

High-temperature solar electricity could also be generated using new technology including solar ponds. This would take into account the local weather which has 300 cloudless days a year. One estimate indicates that the Dead sea itself could support a 450 km^2 solar lake or pond, operating a 2,500 MW power plant, if relatively low saline sea water were made available (Stern and Gradus, 1981). Twenty-first century technology, however, will be needed to make solar energy a reality.

Brackish fossil aquifers have recently been discovered in this area, in and below the Nubian sandstone formation underlying the Negev and Sinai deserts. These aquifers could be tapped in the next century for at least 300×10^6 m^3 per annum of water. The cost of treating this water by reverse osmosis is estimated to be $ 0.30–0.50/m^3 (Murakami, 1991 and 1993b). This unit cost would make it feasible for M and I water use, but not for crop irrigation. However, significant questions remain regarding the sustainability of these brackish fossil aquifers.

The Med-Dead Sea (MDS) Conduit Scheme for Cogeneration

Cogeneration traditionally refers to the use of waste heat from a conventional (oil or coal) energy-producing plant for the desalination of sea water by the distillation method. The co-generation scheme was first conceived to provide both hydro-electricity and freshwater from reverse osmosis sea water desalination plants in the early 1980s (Glueckstern, 1982). The use of a portion of the potential hydro-power to make reverse osmosis desalination cost-effective at the time was put aside, however, owing to its cost and a poor understanding of membrane technologies.

Discussion of the MDS in the early 1980s, given political limitations of the time, may not have sufficiently emphasized the concept of shared resources and the benefits of joint development. The new scheme proposed herein would comprehensively develop the Jordan river system including linkage of the MDS and the Al-Wahde dam on the Yarmouk in addition to other smaller streams flowing into the Jordan river and the Dead sea.

No previous attempt has been made to regionally link sources of both power and water. The key to this approach incorporates both electricity available through a regional grid and hydro-static pressure from the drop to the Dead sea, and takes into account recent innovative developments in membrane technology for reverse osmosis (RO) desalination which saves energy and makes RO desalination more cost-effective. It also recognizes recent changes in the Middle East political situation following the Gulf War in March 1991, the Israel-PLO Declaration of Principles in October 1993 (Israel/PLO, 1993), and the Israel-Jordan Peace Accord and Treaty in August and October 1994. These political actions make comprehensive basin development not only technically and financially feasible, but politically desirable, for the need for co-operative efforts to provide additional water has now become even more urgent.

Hydro-powered sea water Reverse Osmosis (RO) Desalination for Co-generation

The new co-generation scheme would exploit the elevation difference of 400 m between the Mediterranean sea and Dead sea (Fig. 6-2). Inflow to the Dead sea should balance evaporation. The water level of the Dead sea would be maintained at a steady-state with seasonal fluctuations of about 2 metres resulting from surface evaporation. Sea level would thus be sustained between 392.5 m and 390.5 m.

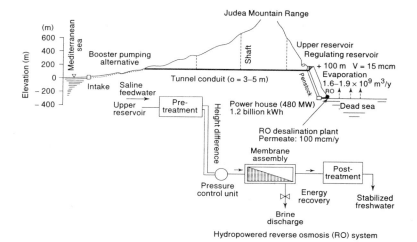

Hydropowered reverse osmosis (RO) system

Fig. 6-2: Schematic Diagram and Profile of MDS Conduit
Scheme for Cogeneration

A possible bi or trilateral development plan involving Israel, Palestine and Jordan in a Mediterranean-Dead sea conduit scheme (IJPMDS) would be a cogeneration alternative which could combine a hydro-electric power scheme with a hydro-powered sea water reverse osmosis (RO) desalination plant (Fig. 6-2). The IJPMDS scheme would have six major structural components, including:

1) an upstream reservoir (the Mediterranean) at zero sea level, with an essentially infinite amount of water,

2) a sea water carrier by tunnel, canal, and pipeline, with a booster pumping station,

3) an upper reservoir and surge shaft at the outlet of the seawater carrier to allow regulating water flow,

4) a storage type hydro-electric unit capable of reverse operation to allow the system to also work as a pumped-storage unit, if required,

5) a downstream reservoir (the Dead sea,) at its present surface elevation of approximately 400m below sea level, and

6) A hydro-powered reverse osmosis (RO) desalination plant, including a pre-treatment unit, a pressure converter unit, the RO unit, an energy recovery unit, a post-treatment unit, and regulating reservoirs for distribution of the resulting freshwater.

Estimates of Hydro-power Potential

The theoretical hydro-potential gained from exploiting the head difference between the Mediterranean sea (0 m) and Dead sea (-400 m) by diverting 56.7 m³/s (1.6 × 10⁹m³ per annum) of sea water is estimated to be 194 MW. The hydro-power plant would produce 1.3 × 10⁹ kWh per annum of electricity with an installed capacity at 495 MW assuming peak-power operation. These figures coincide with the Tahal US plan in 1981 (Tahal Israel, 1982).

Estimates of the hydro-potential are based on equations as shown:

(1) $Pth = (9.8)(Ws)(Q)(He)$
(2) $P = (Pth)(Ef)$
(3) $Pp = (P)(24/8)$
(4) $Wp = (365)(24)(Gf)(P)$

where, Pth: Theoretical hydro-potential (kw)
Ws: Specific weight of sea water (=1.03)
Q: Flow discharge (m³/sec.)
He: Effective difference head of water (m)
P: Installed capacity (kw)
Ef: Synthesized efficiency (=0.85)
Pp: Installed capacity (Assuming 8 hrs/day peak operation)(kw)
Wp: Potential power generation (output) per annum (kWh)

Methods of Cogeneration for the MDS

A booster pumping alternative can be applied to make an effective head difference of 500m. This takes into account an operating water pressure of 50 kg/cm² and cheap electricity during off-peak times. Sea water diversion capacity is estimated to be 50 m³/s, including 39 m³/s of intake water for the hydro-power unit and 11 m³/s of feed water for the desalination unit.

The hydro-power unit would have a theoretical hydro-potential of 160 MW, and would generate 1.2 × 10⁹kWh per annum of electricity with an installed capacity of 480 MW for peak-power operation for 8 hours a day. The installed capacity of the RO plant to produce 100 × 10⁶m³ per annum of permeate is estimated to be

322,300 m^3/d with a load factor of 85 per cent (Murakami, 1991 and 1993a).

Marginal operation for RO is designed to use the system's hydro-potential energy in a penstock having 481.5 m of effective head. The unit would operate for 16 hours a day. The recovered energy (electricity) of 168×10^6 kwh per year from the brine reject water will be used to supply the post-treatment process or other purposes and will thus save electricity that might otherwise be taken from the national grid (Murakami, 1994).

A preliminary estimate of the project cost of the proposed RO unit is $ 389,355,000 for development capital and $ 44,387,000 per annum for O & M. The cost estimates are based on 1990 prices assuming that 1) plant life of 20 years, 2) membrane life (replacement) of 3 years, 3) 8 per cent interest during three years construction, 4) excluding cost-benefits from energy recovery and 5) excluding costs for source water and pipeline/distribution (Murakami, 1991 and 1993a).

THE AQABA HYBRID PUMPED-STORAGE SCHEME WITH HYDRO-POWERED SEA WATER REVERSE OSMOSIS (RO) DESALINATION

Construction of any new thermal and/or nuclear power stations in the region will benefit from a pumped-storage scheme for efficient energy use during off-peak time. Hybrid water-energy co-generation is an application of sea water pumped-storage with reverse osmosis (RO) desalination (Murakami, 1993b). The Aqaba scheme would use sea water which would be pumped directly during off peak time to an upper reservoir on the top of an escarpment at 600 m above sea level, and from there into a penstock yielding an effective water pressure of 55 kg/cm^2 at the end of the pipe. This would generate 600 MW of peak electricity, simultaneously producing 100×10^6 m^3/yr of fresh potable water (Murakami 1994). Off-peak electricity to boost the sea water up to the 600 m elevation would be supplied not only from a steam power plant at Aqaba but also from the most economical alternative sources whether steam or nuclear power plants in Egypt and Israel, or from other sources on the regional electric grid.

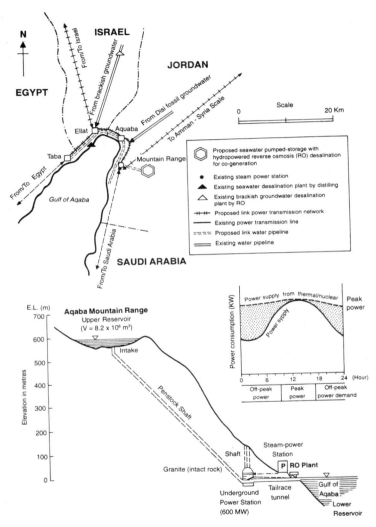

Fig. 6-3: Schematics of Aqaba Hybrid Sea water Pumped-up storage Scheme with Hydro-powered RO Desalination

> ### *Aqaba pumped storage (Technical Details)*
>
> The feed sea water requirements for producing $100 \times 10^6 m^3$ permeate (i.e., freshwater produced by its having permeated an RO membrane) per annum with 1,000 mg/l of the total dissolved solids (TDS) are estimated to be $333 \times 10^6 m^3$ per annum, assuming a 30 per cent recovery is an application of sea water pumped-storage with reverse osmosis ratio. The brine reject of $233 \times 10^6 m^3$ per annum, with a salinity of 57,000 mg/l of TDS, would then be released into the Dead sea (Murakami 1991, 1993c and 1994). The potential energy recovery (PER) from the brine reject is estimated to be 28,280 kw, assuming 20 per cent friction loss in RO circuit as shown below.
>
> Per=$9.8 \times 1.03 \times (233 \times 10^6/365/86400) \times (587 \times 0.95 \times 0.8) \times 0.85$
>
> The annual product of electricity from the RO brine is estimated

> ### *Cost Estimates of the Hydro-powered Reverse Osmosis Desalination Plant*
>
> The per unit water cost of hydro-powered sea water reverse osmosis desalination for the annual product water of $100 \times 10^6 m^3$ is estimated to be $ 0.68/m^3$, which may be reasonable when compared with international water tariffs, e.g. , an estimated per unit water cost of $ 0.85–1.07/m^3$ for the 'Peace Pipeline' Project (David, 1991), and/or ii) estimated per unit water costs of $1.60/m^3$ by conventional reverse osmosis desalination using electricity from the national grid to produce pressures of 50–60 kg/cm² (Murakami 1993b). The recovered energy would be used to supply electricity for the post-treatment or to other pumps, thus replacing electricity taken from the national grid.

A schematic profile of the cogenerating sea water pumped-storage scheme is shown in Fig. 6-3. The design and specification for the hydro-powered sea water reverse osmosis desalination unit would be similar to that developed for the MDS conduit scheme for co-generation.

The marginal operation programme to optimize hydro-power generation and desalination is shown in Fig. 6-4.

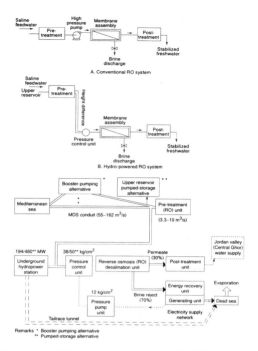

Fig. 6-4: Marginal Operation Programme for Hydro-powered Generation and RO Desalination

Cost Estimates and Water Economy

The cost of a unilateral 600 MW pumped-storage scheme is estimated to be \$ 1.0×10^9 at 1990 prices. The total investment cost of the proposed hydro-powered sea water reverse osmosis (RO) desalination plant is preliminarily estimated to be US\$ 389 million. The annual cost is estimated to be \$ 18.5 million in financing major capital cost elements and \$ 44.4 million in operation and maintenance (O & M) elements as shown in Table 6-1.

The costs of water thus produced has been examined in order to compare the unilateral pumped-storage scheme and the hybrid pumped-storage scheme with RO desalination. The annual benefit of the hybrid scheme is 1.4 times greater than the uni-lateral scheme, assuming tariffs of \$0.10/kWh of peak electricity and \$1.00/m³ of fresh potable water. The cost and benefit elements are shown in Table 6-1.

The preliminary estimate of the per unit water cost of desalination to produce $100 \times 10^6 m^3$ per annum of freshwater from the RO plant is \$0.63 to \$0.74/m³, by assuming the same design criteria and recovery unit including 175×10^6 kwh per year of electricity from the brine reject water.[5] The economy of this method can be seen when compared with either $ 1.60–2.70/m^3 for conventional desalination such as for RO and MSF or the unilateral hydro-power scheme (Murakami, 1991).

Table 6-1: COST AND BENEFITS—THE UNILATERAL AND HYBRID SCHEMES

Feed-water $10^6 m^3/s$	Electri-city 10^6kWh/yr	Permeate $10^6 m^3$/yr	Output/Sale $10^6$$/yr	Project Cost $10^6$$	Annual cost $10^6$$	Capital	O & M	Total Difference
Unilateral Pumped-storage:								
HP 50 1,482		–	148.2	1,000	100.0	5.0	105.0	+43.2
Hybrid Pumped-storage with RO:								
HEe 1,156		–	139.6	905	78.0	5.0	83.0	39
RO 11 (203)		100	100.0	390	37.2	44.4	81.6	
Total 50 1,359		100	239.6	1,295	113.2	49.4	162.6	+ 76.4

Method of Sharing Resources and Benefits

Fresh potable water amounting to $100 \times 10^6 m^3$ per annum from the Aqaba hydro-powered reverse osmosis (RO) desalination plant in the pumped-storage scheme could be shared among Jordan (Aqaba), Israel (Eilat), Egypt (Taba) and Saudi Arabia (Haq-l) in accordance with a possible agreement within the inter-state regional economic development programme. The non-oil producing state of Jordan, the national economy of which is not as strong as those of Israel and Saudi Arabia, would have an exclusive chance to export $100 \times 10^6 m^3$ per annum of fresh, potable water. It would also be able to export valuable peak electricity as well as importing cheap off-peak electricity from Israel, Egypt and Saudi Arabia.

The Aqaba hydro-powered sea water desalination plant will also save $17.5 \times 10^6 m^3$ of fossil ground water currently being pumped from the Disi aquifer to Aqaba for its municipal water supply. A schematic illustration of the method of sharing water and energy from the Aqaba hybrid sea water pumped-storage scheme with the hydro-powered reverse osmosis (RO) desalination system is presented in Fig. 6-3, which assumes the following inter-state cooperation scenarios;

1) An Inter-state electricity grid or network including Egypt, Israel, Palestine, Jordan, Saudi Arabia is incorporated in the plan to transfer inexpensive off-peak electricity, night and morning, to the pumped-storage scheme (buying) and to deliver valuable, day and evening peak electricity to neighbour states (selling).

2) An inter-state water pipeline system connecting three states (Egypt, Israel and Jordan) along the Aqaba coastline is constructed in order to share potable water from the hydro-powered reverse osmosis desalination plant at Aqaba , Jordan.

3) An inter-state sanitation and water environment management programme, which includes treated wastewater recovery for tree crop irrigation as well as protecting the clean water environment of Aqaba bay will be incorporated in the plan. The application of membrane separation technology, including micro-filter (MF) and/or ultra-filter (UF) techniques, will also be adopted in tertiary waste water treatment to reuse for limited irrigation (Murakami, 1994).

CO-OPERATION-INDUCING STAGES OF IMPLEMENTATION IN THE FRAMEWORK OF A REGIONAL WATER DEVELOPMENT PLAN

Negotiations underway in late 1994 and the winter of 1995 indicate the growing possibility of co-operative projects between Israel and the Arab states. Once legal and economic foundations have been laid for the ownership and distribution of current sources of water, and the existing water supply and demand system is functioning at maximum efficiency, a project with the scope of a Med-Dead or Red-Dead canal and Aqaba hybrid pumped-storage scheme could begin to be implemented. In order to achieve a maximum return from such efforts a comparison of the four feasibility elements: technology, environment, economy and politics (Murakami 1991, Wolf 1992, Wolf and Murakami 1994) must take place.

At this point it will be vital to approach a unified solution to water problems in the core area by recognizing three stages of technological applications, 1) short-term (water conservation and re-use, thermal desalination plants), 2) mid-term (water transfer by tankers or bags, Med-Red/Red-Dead canals or hybrid-pumped storage schemes), and 3) long-term (water transfer by inter-state, large scale pipeline schemes). During this process economic, technical and environmental feasibilities should be constantly be reviewed, and the completion of each step taken as inducement for co-operation leading to completion of the whole.

As discussed in Chapter 5, the projects, ranked from earlier to newer ideas, include:

1. Mediterranean to Dead sea (Med-Dead)canal,
2. Red sea to Dead sea (Red-Dead)canal,
3. Pumped Storage, including Aqaba, the eastern and western shores of the Dead sea, and the eastern shore of the sea of Galilee,
4. Jordan valley salt drainage canal, and
5. Desalination.

It is now possible to suggest a time schedule for the application of the several technologies.

SHORT- TO MID-TERM SCHEME: IMMEDIATE STEPS

The first phase should begin immediately now that post peace negotiations between the PLO and Israel and Jordan and Israel are in progress. To cope with short- and mid-term urgent needs to supply water in Gaza, the most parched of the areas under discussion, a traditional, small-scale coal or oil-fired, dual-purpose energy/desalination plant or RO plant could be built on the Gazan shore (Murakami 1991; 1994; Murakami and Wolf 1994). The authors recognize the complexity of this situation and appreciate the detailed suggestions made elsewhere regarding an overall solution (Baskin 1994; Elmusa, 1994). Baskin, for example (guideline # 14, p. 33) suggests the immediate return of the safe yield of the Gaza aquifer (60 mcm/yr) to the Palestinians. While this act would go far to relieve the catastrophic water situation there, it would not suffice; therefore, the authors view their suggestions as meshing with, rather than contradicting many other related ideas.

The second priority area (taking into account the peace agreement between Israel and Jordan) in order to implement the suggested inter-state economic co-operation programme should be the Aqaba pumped storage project. At the same time, the feasibility of this project for joint use among Jordan, Israel, Egypt and Saudi Arabia should be examined. This review would take into account 1) energy savings, particularly in the form of fuel oil, and the positive impact of such reductions on the local and global environment, 2) long-term flexible supplies of peak electricity and freshwater, and 3) a reduction of political constraints as well as increasing geo-political and economic incentives for Jordan.

This facility would be designed for initial incorporation into the Med-Dead or Red-Dead canal projects. Co-ordination with other potential core projects is important in order to proceed rationally to the next phase. Both the Aqaba hybrid pumped-storage and Med-Dead sea canal would be ideally suited for development in such a step-wise fashion, dependent upon increasing confidence-building incentives. These projects also could be designed to be expanded, in order to incorporate additional components as future power and water needs grow, and to have a flexible capacity to re-allocate outputs and benefits corresponding to long-term changes in water and electricity demands.

MID- TO LONG-TERM SCHEME: A BASIN MASTER PLAN FOR THE JORDAN RIVER SYSTEM

Projects such as solar-powered desalination, hydro-powered reverse osmosis desalination, aquaculture, and inland commerce and industry in the area would become feasible with the linkage by conduit of the Mediterranean or Red sea to the Dead sea. Once intake and power generation facilities with or without RO desalination plants were in place, even under different sovereignties, the incentive to connect the various facilities, and later to develop consequent ancillary projects would be powerful enough to induce ever-increasing co-operation.

Storage capacity in the Dead sea basin for the MDS canal scheme for cogeneration should be considered a joint resource of the lacustrian states: Israel (300 km^2; 30 per cent), Jordan and Palestine (700 km^2; 70 per cent). Evaporation rates from the Dead sea's surface after impounding sea water from the Mediterranean have been estimated to be 1,908 mm per annum (Calder and Neal, 1984). This would allow a water budget for a Dead sea cogeneration scheme generating 1.2×10^9 kWh per annum of electricity and $100 \times 10^6 m^3$ per annum of freshwater (Murakami, 1991; Biswas, et al., 1994) (Table 6-2).

Table 6-2: WATER BUDGET OF THE DEAD SEA WITH
NON-CONVENTIONAL TECHNO-POLITICAL ALTERNATIVE SCHEMES

Flow Balance	Million Cubic Metre (mcm) per year			
	before 1948	after 1967	pls MDS	pls MDS + PDC
Ground elevation below sea level (m)	E.L.-391	E.L.-406	E.L.-391	E.L.-392
Surface area of the Dead sea (km²)	1,000	900	1,000	1,000
Annual flow potential from the whole catchment	1,600	1,600	1,600	1,600
Inflow from catchment of the Jordan river	1,100	400	224 *	211 *
Inflow from catchment of the Dead sea	500	400	223 *	211 *
Abstraction of flow from the whole catchment	nil	800	1,153 *	1,178 *
Evaporation from the Dead sea surface	-1,600	-1,500		
Evaporation after impounding seawater from Mediterranean sea			-1,900	-1,900
Tailrace water from MDS hydro-power station			1,220	1,220
Brine reject water from RO plant in MDS			233	233
Brine reject water from RO plant in PDC				25
Inflow potential from the whole catchment	1,600	800	447	422
Inflow potential from the whole catchment	0	-700	0	0

Note: Above figures are approximate water budget in mcm per year.
    E.L.-391m had been a historical equilibrium water level of the Dead sea before 1930–48
    It will take several decades to fill up the Dead sea with seawater at the historical equilibrium level (1,600–2,000 mcm).
* These figures are some residual flows from the catchment which could be developed in the future stage.

The water budget of the Dead sea indicates that a decrease in inflow from the Jordan river catchment would allow the additional introduction of Mediterranean water, thereby increasing the system's hydro-potential energy.

There are four main alternatives to cut the flows from the Jordan river catchment: In all cases the impounded or desalinized water reclaimed by these projects would be put to use, with negligible return flow to the Dead sea.

1) The Al-Wahde storage dam on the Yarmouk river, (or dams in Syrian territory upstream).

2) Storage dam schemes on the rift side-wadis on the East Bank, including Wadi Mujib and Wadi Hasa.

3) Flood retention-groundwater recharge dam schemes on the

Table 6-3: TECHNO-POLITICAL ASSESSMENT SHEET FOR THE DEAD SEA AND THE AQABA SCHEMES BEFORE AND AFTER 26 OCTOBER 1994

Techno-political alternatives	Technical feasibility				Environmental feasibility	Economic feasibility			Political feasibility	Total
	Quantity	Quality	Reliability	Sub-total		Financial viability	Benefit /cost	Sub-total		
Weight (%)	12.5	5.0	7.5	25.0	25.0	12.5	12.5	25.0	25.0	100
1. After the 'Treaty of Peace' between Jordan and Israel on 26 October, 1994										
Lower Jordan river 'Peace Drainage Canal' with RO desalination	31.0	66.0	62.0	47.3	55.8	61.0	61.0	61.0	69.0	58.3
Aqaba pumped-storage scheme with hydro-powered seawater RO desalination	32.5	68.8	57.5	47.3	45.0	52.9	53.6	53.3	53.0	49.6
MDS hydro-solar development with hydro-powered seawater RO desalination	40.0	72.5	60.0	52.5	45.0	33.8	48.3	41.1	35.3	43.5
Dead sea pumped-storage	15.0	30.0	60.0	31.5	40.0	53.3	40.0	46.7	46.7	41.2
Mediterranean-Dead sea canal, without RO desalination	23.8	31.3	61.3	36.6	22.5	36.3	30.0	33.2	38.5	32.7
Red-Dead sea canal without RO desalination	21.3	30.0	28.8	25.3	22.5	33.8	30.0	31.9	44.2	31.0

Techno-political alternatives	Technical feasibility				Environmental feasibility	Economic feasibility			Political feasibility	Total
	Quantity	Quality	Reliability	Sub-total		Financial viability	Benefit /cost	Sub-total		
Weight (%)	12.5	5.0	7.5	25.0	25.0	12.5	12.5	25.0	25.0	100
2. Before the 'Treaty of Peace' between Jordan and Israel on 26 October, 1994										
Lower Jordan river 'Peace Drainage Canal' with RO desalination	31.0	66.0	62.0	47.3	55.8	61.0	61.0	61.0	69.0	58.3
Aqaba pumped-storage scheme with hydro-powered seawater RO desalination	32.5	68.8	57.5	47.3	26.3	37.0	37.5	37.3	24.0	33.7
MDS hydro-solar development with hydro-powered seawater RO desalination	40.0	72.5	60.0	52.5	45.0	33.8	33.8	33.8	35.3	41.7
Dead sea pumped-storage	15.0	30.0	60.0	31.5	40.0	53.3	40.0	46.7	46.7	41.2
Mediterranean-Dead sea canal, without RO desalination	23.8	31.3	61.3	36.6	22.5	36.3	30.0	33.2	38.5	32.7
Red-Dead sea canal without RO desalination	21.3	30.0	28.8	25.3	22.5	33.8	30.0	31.9	31.0	27.7

Note: After 'Treaty of Peace' between Jordan and Israel on 26 October, 1994, some details on the cost estimates and environment impact analysis were added by M. Murakami. Assessment sheet before the 'Treaty of Peace', *see* the original (Wolf and Murakami 1994, Ref. 13) side-wadis on the West Bank (Occupied Palestine) and the Judean mountain range where limestone geology predominates.

4) Salvaging saline water including saline springs and irrigation return in the lower Jordan system between the Sea of Galilee and the Dead sea, by installing a 'Salt Drainage/Peace canal' 85 km long leading to a brackish water reverse osmosis (RO) desalination plant with an installed capacity of $75 \times 10^6 m^3$ per annum at the terminus of the Jordan river mainstream.

Among the above, the Al-Wahde dam scheme with an effective storage of $195 \times 10^6 m^3$, is Jordan's last major river development, and is urgently needed. This would add $155 \times 10^6 m^3$ per annum (or in less then 12 months) of renewable freshwater to the national water supply grid. The storage of winter flow will also reduce substantial amounts of discharge into the Dead sea. This could add 20 MW of hydro-potential (120×10^6 kWh per annum of electricity) (Murakami, 1993c). The product water of $100 \times 10^6 m^3$ per annum could be split equally between Israel, Palestine and Jordan. This water would be mainly used for M & I water supplies with the aim of supplying fresh potable water exclusively in the hot and arid low lands of the Jordan valley. (No pumping to higher elevations is recommended.)

Taking into account the new political implications of the Treaty of Peace between Jordan and Israel (26 October 1994), and recent evaluations of costs and environmental impact for the cogeneration schemes, a techno-political assessment was made in order to identify new priorities (as shown in Table 6-3). As a result, three such schemes have been assigned mid-term priority: the Jordan valley salt drainage/peace canal, the Aqaba hybrid sea water pumped storage for Cogeneration Plan, and the MDS conduit for cogeneration.

This study assigns first priority to the Jordan valley salt drainage canal (SDC) as an environmentally sound desalination option which would salvage $75 \times 10^6 m^3/yr$ of saline or brackish waters in the lower Jordan system (Figs. 5 and 6). The SDC and desalination plant would not only protect the water quality of the lower main stream, but would also supply new potable water from the brackish water it diverts. The per unit cost of this water would be $ 0.48/m^3$.

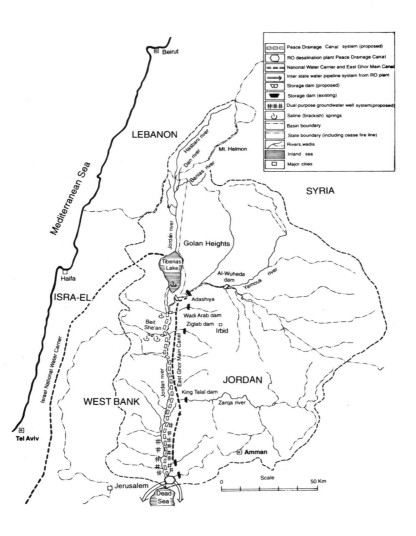

Fig. 6-5: Jordan River System and 'Salt/Peace Drainage Canal' Scheme

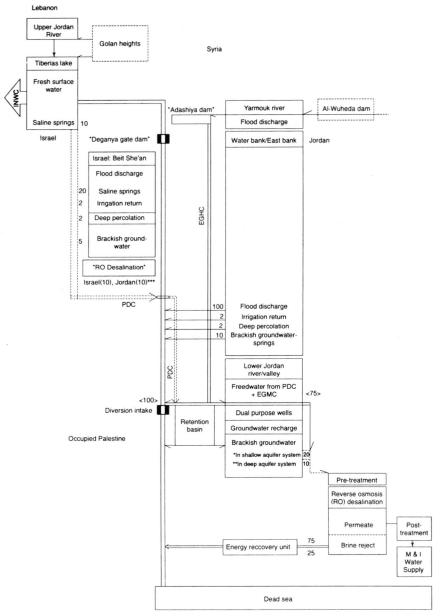

Remarks:

PDC: Peace Drainage Canal, EGMC: East Ghor Main Canal, INWC: Israel National Water Carrier

100, <100>: Unit in Million Cubic Meter

Plans in "Treaty of Peace" in October 1994 including "Adashiya dam", "Deganya gate dam", and "RO desalination plant" in Israel

  *Brackish groundwater in shallow saquifer : Summer period

  **Brackish groundwater in deep aquifer   : Drought period

  ***Water allocation of RO permeate in "Treaty of Peace" of October 1994

CONCLUSIONS

The above plan, which includes the two strategic regions of the Dead sea and the Gulf of Aqaba, has attempted to evaluate some new non-conventional approaches to water resource management, which need to taken into account during the search for peace in the core of the Middle East.

Although costs have long been a constraint in considering sea water desalination, hydro-powered sea water reverse osmosis (RO) desalination in the Aqaba hybrid pumped-storage scheme would achieve substantial cost reductions by retrieving off-peak electricity from steam power plants elsewhere in the region. The per unit water cost of hydro-powered sea water RO desalination is preliminarily estimated to be $ 0.63–0.74/m^3, which is 50 per cent or less than the cost of traditional RO ($ 1.68/m^3) or MSF ($ 2.7/m^3).[6]

Regardless of whether the Red-Dead or the Med-Dead plan is chosen, the Dead sea hydro-conduit development for cogeneration should be discussed in the context of a basin water master plan for sustainable development and management This should be based on the concept of sharing resources in order to provide the basis for peaceful collaboration between Israel and its neighbours.

The Aqaba hybrid pumped-storage scheme with hydro-powered sea water reverse osmosis desalination would be a feasible core project in an inter-state region including Jordan, Israel and Palestine, and with the possible integration of Egypt and Saudi Arabia. A comparative technical-political feasibility study including non-conventional alternatives should be carried out within the framework of an inter-state regional development master plan.

The new approaches described above offer an opportunity to introduce new applications of well-tried technology in order to solve long-standing water and energy problems that are possible sources of potential conflict. As the Romans established a *Pax Romanum*, so may imaginative water management provide a *Pax Aquarum* for the Middle East.

In the more distant future, population may well increase to a degree where even the minimization of agricultural water demands will fail to meet domestic and industrial water needs. At that time, not only sea water desalination but also water imports from the periphery may become critical, particularly for inland locations in Jordan and Syria.

Because such projects are of even greater complexity than those suggested for the core, their evaluation and planning should start now if imported waters are to be available in twenty to thirty years time. Until then, it must not be forgotten that the storage capacity of the Dead sea is fixed by economic, social and political constraints as well as by nature, and that unlimited amounts of water cannot be poured into its basin. This limitation has been considered in the scheme presented above and is shown in Table 6-3. It is further examined in Chapter 7 where import of water from the periphery is considered.

NOTES

1. See ISPAN, *Gulf of Aqaba Environmental Data Survey*, for a full description of intended developments in this area.
2. Current activity is focused upon the RSDS scheme. The authors feel, however, that the MDS project also should be considered. Technical and geological constraints associated with the RSDS project are discussed below.
3. See ISPAN, *Gulf of Aqaba* .
4. Assuming a gross water head of 444 to 472 m and a maximum discharge of 200 m^3/sec and an annual average flow intake of $1.23–1.67×10^9 m^3$ (Tahal Israel, 1982).
5. It should be noted that the optional use of $100 × 10^6 m^3$ feed water in the hydro-power sector would generate $143 × 10^9$ kWh per annum of electricity or a $ $5.91 × 10^6$ potential shadow benefit (Output/Sales-Cost). The estimated per unit water cost of the hydro-powered sea water RO desalination is $ $0.69/m^3$($= 0.63 + 0.059$).
5. The cost of $0.74 includes the cost-benefit return of using sea water for hydro-power generation rather than RO.

7 Inter-unit Transfers from the Periphery to the Core

INTRODUCTION

Cost does not stop water projects. Water projects are often extravagant. Every drop of water used in the western United States is subsidized. The Colorado river desalination plant which sends cleaner water to Mexico is outrageously expensive when the alternative of retiring saline upstream fields is considered. Agriculture in the Central Valley of California exists only through taxpayer subsidies. Proponents of the proposed Three Gorges Dam on the Yellow river in China do not count its true costs.[1] The swimming pools of Los Angeles and Haifa would never have opened if the pumping costs of water were fully paid by their users. The agricultural programmes of every nation in the Mashreq cannot be justified on the basis of water costs, and yet they flourish.

Politics start and stop water projects. The 'rights' of American farmers and the fate of their congressional representatives are nourished by costly water. American relations with Mexico are in part guaranteed or imperiled by the quality of Colorado river water. The monolithic regime in China is celebrated by its technical monuments. And the aquatic recreation of the populace is ensured by vote hungry politicians.

Are these statements too cynical or unrealistic? Or would a dose of real politik cut through much of the confusion and delay surrounding regional water problems in the Middle East? The cost of one day's war exceeds any but the largest of water projects, and the pecuniary concern of European and American economists with regard to differences of a few cents in the costs per cubic metre of Middle Eastern water seem strange when compared to the hydro-follies found in their own countries.

The proposal which follows for linking the periphery, with its more abundant water supplies, to the needy core falls well within the technical and financial range of existing worldwide water projects. Its authors recognize the complexity surrounding such issues and present their ideas solely as an heuristic example of the type of long-term collaborative options that should be considered in attempting to solve the water problems of the Mashreq and its core. We do not propose that this is the answer, but hope that the following presentation will stimulate productive thinking on ways to approach periphery to core hydrologic relations.

The underlying principle with which our proposal has been conceived is one of political practicality. The best bargain is one where both sides feel they have gained. As will be indicated, every country involved would gain something it wants and would give up nothing it has, with the exception of Turkey which would receive both monetary and technical compensation for sharing a surplus commodity. The mutually satisfying inter-linkages would also go far to ensure the continued functioning of the system once in place. Moreover, the suggested system would augment, rather than interfere with, the plans for the core suggested in the preceding chapters.

SUGGESTED CONVEYANCES—PERIPHERY TO CORE

During past decades numerous proposals intended to alleviate water shortages in the Mashreq by means of imported water have been made. None of these have been accepted or put in place, but neither have those ideas disappeared. Therefore, with increasing need for supplemental water supplies and the slow resolution of project inhibiting political differences the possibility exists that one or more such schemes may find the light of day. A brief description of each of these major proposals follows in order to familiarize the reader with their attributes. To our knowledge no reliable cost/feasibility studies exist for the listed schemes, but such an omission does not rule out their eventually being made operable.

The schemes described are (Fig. 7-1):

1. A pipeline from the Iraqi Euphrates to Jordan,
2. President Ozal's Turkish peace pipeline,
3. A mini-peace pipeline,
4. A mini-mini peace pipeline,
5. A Golan Heights peace canal,
6. The trans-Syria pipeline,

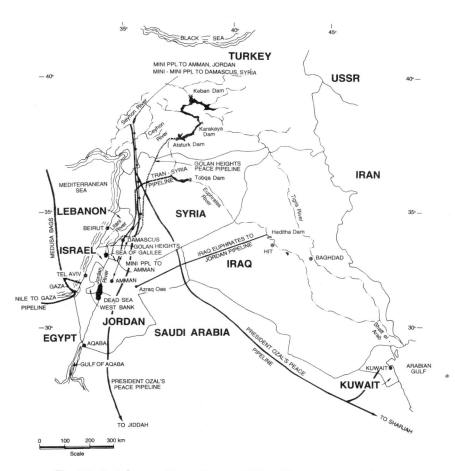

Fig. 7-1: Periphery to Core—**Proposed** Water Transportation Schemes

7. Medusa Bags (sea borne),
8. A Nile to Gaza pipeline. (*See* box below).

Similar ideas have been suggested in order to bring water directly to the GCC countries. While these will not be presented here, they include pipelines from Iran to Bahrein and/or Qatar, Iraq to Kuwait, and Pakistan (the Indus River) to the UAE. Similar to these is the suggested Nile to Gaza Pipeline which is included here but not in our analysis for the reasons stated above (Footnote 2, Chap. 1).

Nile to Israel Pipeline

Egypt's El-Salaam Canal/Pipeline is proposed to bring between 2,800 mcm/yr (for the first 26 km) and 1,500 mcm/yr (to El-Arish) in the northern Sinai. To meet the suggested Nile to Gaza requirements the capacity of the canal would have to be increased by 500 mcm/yr as well as extending its length 50 km to Gaza and another 15 km to Ashkelon. The total cost of this project has been estimated to be $695 million (1984 prices). Israel, upon receiving Nile water, might release an equivalent amount to Jordan or the Palestinians from the northern Jordan or the West Bank.

The offer of Egyptian water was first made by Anwar Sadat in 1981 in the face of resistance to the idea by both Israeli and Palestinian nationalists. Acceptance of substitute waters in place of those originating on the West Bank is deemed unacceptable by most Palestinians. Such an action, they feel, would indicate acceptance of the territorial *status quo*.

Another major objection to this project is that the inter-basin transfer of Nile waters would in the long run have to be approved by the ten co-riparians on the river. It should also be noted that Nile waters as of December 1994 had yet to cross the Suez canal.

Euphrates–Jordan Pipeline

This is the first such scheme to be considered. Sir Hamilton Gibb and Company suggested that a pipeline be run from the Euphrates river in Iraq as far as Amman, Jordan. The original idea may have been based on the existence, at that time, of the TAP petroleum pipeline, for water would be pumped from the river into a pipeline which would follow an existing but unused oil pipeline across western Iraq and Northern Jordan. The line would terminate near the Azraq oasis and thereafter the water would flow to Irbid and Amman through an existing system. The line would have been about 610 km in length and would divert about 160 mcm/yr to Jordan. No cost estimates are available for this project, but based on an approximate unit cost of pipe installed, the cost would be about $1.8 billion.

The project was never carried out. Iraq's position *vis-à-vis* other Arab states makes it politically unviable. Perhaps more significant is the uncertainty surrounding the quantity and quality of water in the Euphrates river at the point of removal. These will depend upon developments upstream in Turkey and Syria.

President Özal's Peace Pipeline

In 1987 Prime Minister (later President) Türgut Özal proposed a 'Peace Pipeline' (PPL) intended to alleviate water shortages of Turkey's southern neighbours. The PPL would carry as much as 3.5 thousand m^3 water daily (1.28×10^9 m^3/yr) from the Seyhan and Ceyhan rivers in two lines. The western PPL would reach Jiddah in Saudi Arabia, and the eastern PPL would extend as far as Sharjah in the UAE. The contracting firm of Brown and Root at that time estimated a cost between $17 billion and $20 billion.

While technologically feasible, the offer evoked no official and scant private response from the potential recipients. The Arab memories of Ottoman rule combined with scepticism regarding the political reliability of a line's crossing so many intervening borders essentially vetoed the PPL's success. Questions regarding the amount and quality of the water sources also were raised, though subsequent conversations with GAP engineers by the present authors indicate that the headwaters of the Seyhan River should be able to provide the indicated amount (Kolars and Mitchell, 289–97; Kolars, in Bagis, 1994, 129–53). Cost considerations were mentioned in passing, but played little part in the rejection of the PPL.

A Mini Peace Pipeline

A shorter version of the peace pipeline was suggested by Kolars in 1991 at a World Bank seminar on water management (Kolars, World Bank,

1992). Based on President Özal's original proposal, this mini-peace pipeline would carry approximately 600 mcm water to Syria and as far as Amman, Jordan. Its cost would be proportionately less than the PPL, and the amount of water delivered smaller. Syria and Jordan would be the direct beneficiaries, although a domino effect might take place downstream on the Yarmouk river, making water available to Palestinians on the West Bank, and perhaps even to Israel.

This idea entered the growing ranks of periphery to core water projects and while never rejected, it faced the same criticisms as those leveled at the original PPL, although to a lesser degree.

A Mini-mini Pipeline

A mini-mini PPL was suggested by Hillel Shuval as a refinement of the mini-PPL idea. In this case, the line would extend only as far as Damascus and its southern environs. Delivery of its water would, it is hoped, take some pressure off the headwaters of the Yarmouk. The advantage offered by the mini-PPL is that only one border would have to be crossed (Turkey/Syria).

A Golan Heights Peace Canal

The idea of a Golan heights peace canal has been offered by Boaz Wachtel as an effort to both alleviate the water shortages in Syria, Jordan, Palestine and Israel and also as a means of answering questions of occupancy of the Golan Heights. Water for the project would be obtained from Lake Ataturk and would require about 1,100 mcm annually. Pipelines would lead across Turkey and Syria to the existing border between Syria and the Golan Heights. Thereafter, a 60 km open canal, 30 m wide and 3 m deep would lead to the south, forming an effective 'tank barrier'. Two smaller canals, 20 metres wide and 3 m deep, would parallel the main canal. They would carry water in the event of necessary repairs to the large canal as well as serving as buffer tank barriers, thus preventing incursions by either party occupying the heights. Thereafter, the flow would be split, half going to the Sea of Galilee, the other portion falling to the Yarmouk river where it could be stored in the reservoir (to be constructed) behind the Maqarin Dam. In both cases an estimated 700 MW hydroelectric capacity would be generated. Estimated building costs come to $1.5 billion (1994 dollar). No estimates are available for operating costs.

Project facilities would include: a tunnel through the mountains southwest of the Ataturk Dam, twin pipelines from the Ataturk reservoir to the Golan Heights, a lined canal/anti-tank barrier along the heights, and hydro-electric facilities on the Yarmouk river and Lake Tiberius.

Numerous objections have been raised to this scheme in addition to its cost. Primary among such caveats, is the unacceptable assumption that hostilities are inevitable on the Golan Heights, or that at the least, the territory will remain divided, for Syria demands complete return of the Golan as its fee for peace. Others contend that the peace canal would also increase Jordanian and Palestinian dependence on Israel for an uninterrupted flow of water.

The Trans-Syria Pipeline (TSP)

This suggestion represents an idea informally suggested by Syrian officials to the authors as members of the Middle East Water Commission. The TSP would take water from Lake Assad and bring it south by an all Syrian conveyor. Along the way, the major Syrian cities of Aleppo, Homs, and Damascus, would be served. Additional water would be emptied into the headwaters of the Yarmouk for division among Jordan, Palestine, and possibly Israel.[2]

This project differs from all other suggested pipeline schemes in that natural river systems would be used to convey water across international borders. This would satisfy an expressed Syrian desire to limit international boundary involvement. From an economic point of view, although some water would be lost to seepage and evaporation from river and reservoir surfaces, a significant amount of piping and tunneling would be avoided on the route between Turkey and Syria.

The main problems facing such an effort are political. Syrian and Turkish co-operation will depend upon and involve the sharing of waters from the Euphrates, Asi (Orontes), and Tigris Rivers. The water removed from Lake Assad for the TSP would have to be released by Turkey and would be in addition to any Syrian or Iraqi 'equitable share' agreed upon by the three riparians in concert. It should be noted that Iraq, though not an active player at the moment, must still be included to its satisfaction in any riparian settlement.

Medusa Bags

The technology represented in this concept has been developed and refined by James A. Cran.[3] Water from the Manavgat river on the south central coast of Turkey, which now flows unused into the Mediterranean sea, would be taken by pipeline to an offshore loading facility. Thereafter, it would be pumped into large reinforced fabric bags, towed by sea going tugs to the shores of Gaza or Israel and off loaded for use.

These 'Medusa Bags' would each be about 700 m long, 170 m wide, and 20 m deep, and contain about 1.5 mcm. A continuous cycle of full and empty bags assuring a continuous supply of water at the receiving end would require six bags and six tugs.

The total investment cost for the project is estimated to be about $300 million, and the annual cost for operation and maintenance about $12 million. At an interest rate of 12 per cent per annum, the cost of water would be about $0.20/$m^3$, decreasing to about $0.17/$m^3$ at an interest rate of 7.5 per cent.

There seem to be no major technical objections to this scheme save for its untried character. A 5000 m^3 bag has been successfully tested, but further work has been delayed by lack of financing. Politically, the Gazans object to any notion which would indicate that they accept the *status quo* regarding Israeli use of West Bank or other related waters. A counter argument is that if the water were delivered to Israel a similar amount of West Bank water would be released to Gaza. On the other hand, many Israelis object to being dependent on any water from foreign sources. There also remains the question of such sea borne Medusa water's being a practical answer to severe shortages now developing in inland Jordan and Syria.

A somewhat similar scheme, Aquarius linked bags, has been suggested by Christopher Savage. This would entail sea borne, smaller bags towed like links of sausage from Turkey to Israel. Scant information is available regarding this idea.

Given the various schemes described above, it is now possible to attempt the authors' own answer to the question of periphery to core water transfers.

A REGIONAL WISH LIST

Consideration of this periphery to core proposal begins with a list of water related items including something for every unit[4] in the region (Table 7-1).

Table 7-1: DESIRED WATER RELATED GOALS

Turkey	Help with Black sea flood control
	Help with integrated water system to serve western cities
	Additional foreign exchange
	Cooperation with Syria regarding Kurdish question
	Rapprochement concerning waters of the Asi river (Orontes)
	Rapprochement with Syria and Iraq over Euphrates waters
Syria	Rapprochement with Turkey over Euphrates waters
	Means to bring additional water to its cities (Aleppo, Homs, Damascus)
	No water pipelines crossing international borders (This notion has been stated by Syrians in positions of authority—*see* text.)
	Building of a trans-Syria pipeline as part of the urban water solution
	Resolution of Yarmouk headwaters question
Jordan	Additional water from the Yarmouk river
	Augmenting of limited water supplies, particularly to cities
Palestine West Bank	Completion of West Ghor canal with an additional share of water
	Control of the water which falls as precipitation on the West Bank,
	A larger share of the Yarqon-Taninim aquifer
Gaza	Additional supplies of 'Palestinian' water from the West Bank
Israel	Continuing use of its established share of West Bank water
	Additional water supplies for future use with guaranteed integrity

Let us assume 1200 mcm of Turkish water's being delivered from the north. (The quantity specified is somewhat arbitrary and could be increased or diminished depending upon negotiation as could the number of units served). As mentioned above, the absolute constraint upon this assumption is the settling of the issue of sharing Euphrates and Tigris rivers among the three riparians.[5] While at present seemingly intractable, these problems should be no more difficult to solve than those confronting the Arabs and the Israelis, many of which recently have been resolved.

THE ARTICULATED SYSTEM

As shown in Fig. 7-2, 1200 mcm of additional water is released by Turkey downstream in the Euphrates. In return for this water, Turkey receives direct monetary compensation, and/or compensation in combination with an improved situation on the Asi, and/or an acceptable resolution of the Kurdish question *vis-à-vis* Syria, and/or a variety of internal improvements with the technological and financial assistance of the World Bank, or the UN, or the United States, or possibly Israel.

This water is released into the Euphrates river instead of being piped to the south for two reasons. Syrian officials have specifically told members of the Middle East Water Commission that although they do not want water pipelines crossing their borders from Turkey or from Syria to Jordan, the transfer of water via natural channels is acceptable to them. The second reason is financial, no pipeline construction or maintenance expenses would be incurred from the point of entry in Turkey as far as the point of removal from Lake Assad in Syria. This would represent a saving unavailable in previous pipeline proposals.

A trans-Syria pipeline (TSP) would be constructed with the technological and financial help of concerned outsiders. This pipeline would transfer water for Lake Assad south to the headwaters of the Yarmouk river while servicing the main cities of Aleppo, Homs, and Damascus along the way. It should be noted that of the 400 mcm thus allocated, 200 mcm would serve urban areas, in order to relieve a serious and growing deficit therein, and 200 mcm would replace water from the sources of the Yarmouk in Syria which are at present being diverted for use in Syria. The TSP would also be available to transport additional amounts of Syrian water from Lake Assad southward to agricultural areas and/or for additional urban supplies.

The TSP would also be used to ship an additional 800 mcm directly from Lake Assad (67 per cent of the original 1200 mcm) to the Yarmouk river. Of this 800 mcm, 500 mcm would move downstream directly into The Sea of Galilee. It should be noted that the Sea of Galilee would serve only as a channel, not as a reservoir, for this flow, and that an equal amount (*see* below) would be simultaneously

The Periphery to Core Exchange System

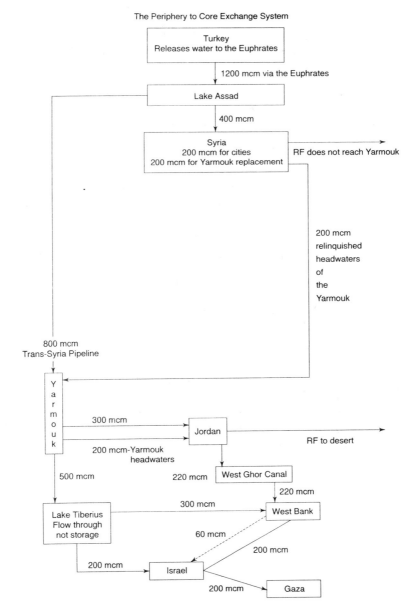

Fig. 7-2: The Periphery to Core Exchange System

removed for further shipment. Little or no additional storage is possible along the Jordan-Yarmouk system, therefore, the water mentioned here might also be scheduled for summer storage only. Jordan would receive the remaining 300 mcm as a much needed supplement.

At the same time, part of the natural flow of the Yarmouk amounting to 200 mcm, which has been replaced for Syria as stated above, reaches Jordan for use as indicated below.

Jordan would therefore receive 500 mcm of water by means of the Yarmouk. Of this amount, 60 mcm can be counted on as return flow (RF). It should be noted that this RF could be directed into the eastern desert where it could augment pasturage for herding, and would not interfere with previously discussed Dead sea hydro-power and sweet water generation plans for the regional core. Thereafter, 220 mcm would be directed to a newly constructed West Ghor Canal, fulfilling a long standing promise to that area. At present this amount of water is not needed in the Jordan valley, but environmental considerations for a healthy Jordan river as well as additonal water for Jordanian and Palestinian farmers and for increased tourism could easily absorb this quantity. Jordan would thus gain use of 340 mcm (Table 7-2 and 7-3).

Table 7-2: WATERS GAINED BY THE KINGDOM OF JORDAN

300 mcm	direct transfer
200 mcm	Yarmouk headwaters
60 mcm	Return Flow (to desert)
560 mcm	Sub total
220 mcm	to West Bank
340 mcm	Used in Jordan

The seaward slope of the West Bank would in turn receive 300 mcm of the 500 mcm sent directly to the Sea of Galilee. This in combination with the 220 mcm from Jordan and some desalinized byproduct (approximately 30 mcm) would give the West Bank 350 mcm for its own use and 200 mcm to pass on to Gaza.

Table 7-3: WATERS GAINED BY THE WEST BANK

20 mcm	from Jordan to West Ghor
300 mcm*	from Sea of Galilee
30 mcm	approximate return from RF desalination (for use in Dead sea valley settlements)
Sub total	550 mcm
-200 mcm	to Gaza
350 mcm	Total for use on the West Bank

Note: * – 60 mcm after use, down slope to Israel; this RF only from 300 mcm sent to the west slope of the West Bank.

Israel would receive 200 mcm directly from The Sea of Galilee for discretionary use (recharge of the coastal aquifer?) and 60 mcm return flow from the West Bank. This water would be in recognition of the West Bank's and Gaza's use of the Israeli NWC, the use of which would ensure that no attempt would be made to cut off Israel's share of these waters.

At the system's terminus, Gaza would obtain 200 mcm of West Bank water (i.e., Palestinian water, perceived as rightfully theirs) via an existing pipeline, another financial saving.

SUMMARY

In summary, comparison of the above schedule with the 'wish list' given in Table 7-1 indicates that many of the listed desires/needs would be fulfilled with no sacrifice on the part of any of the participants. Nor does the introduction of this relatively small amount of water into the core of the region in any way jeopardize the sequence of technological events or choices described in the preceding chapters. More specifically, the proposed scheme would maintain the level of the Dead sea prescribed in Chapter 6.

Construction costs would also be minimized. In place of a longer and more elaborate peace pipe line (PPL), or mini-PPL, or Peace Canal, two shorter, non-international water carriers would be built: the trans-Syria pipeline, and the West Ghor canal (which could take water directly from the Jordan river below its confluence with the Yarmouk), as well as two existing linkages from the Sea of Galilee to the northern part of the seaward slope of the West Bank,[6] and from the Israeli NWC to Gaza.

NOTES

1. *US Water News* (March 1995).
2. This latter inclusion was inferred but not stated; the matter being dependent upon the resolution of the Golan Heights controversy.
3. The authors wish to thank James Cran for these cost estimates.
4. It should be noted that the title which introduces this chapter uses the term 'inter-unit' rather than 'inter-basin' or 'international' to modify the notion of water transfers. The reason for this usage is that with the exception of desalinized water, any new sources of significant quantities of water in the Mashreq must perforce cross the boundaries of nation states as well as natural watersheds in order to reach their points of use. It is counter productive to fret over such perceived transgressions. In the United States individual states, operating under their federal umbrella, allow waters to cross natural and political boundaries with relatively little angst once details have been ironed out and arbitrated at that higher level. No such overarching panacea exists in the Middle East, but a substitute might be found in the concept of linked, mutually rewarding exchanges. It is suggested that thinking in terms of units without political or hydrologic modifiers may allow the discussion to proceed by avoiding nationalistic and/or positional rhetoric.
5. Syria and Iraq have already reached an agreement that 58 per cent of the water of the Euphrates crossing the border from Turkey into Syria will belong to Iraq, and the remaining 42 per cent to Syria. The remaining question is what overall share will be Turkey's and what Syria's and Iraq's? This is complicated by parallel issues regarding allegations by Turkey regarding Syrian support of Kurdish separatists, and Syrian overuse of the waters of the Asi (Orontes) river.
6. This line might not be necessary if a trade off between the waters of the Northeast Aquifer, currently used in the Jezraeel area, were replaced with water from the Sea of Galilee.

8   Epilogue as Prologue

It would be redundant and tedious to recapitulate the detailed descriptions and complex technical suggestions given in the preceding chapters. This epilogue, based upon what this study's authors have encountered, argued about together, and concluded, will attempt instead the briefest glimpse into what they perceive as the role of water in the Middle East.

In summary, our analysis emphasizes 1) the core's high variance in rainfall and the severe limitations on aquifers, 2) the importance of a mixture of hydro-technologies designed to meet the needs of this transitional region, 3) the combined production of hydro-electricity (HE) and reverse osmosis (RO) water, 4) the use of off-peak electricity for pumped storage to meet peak demand electric generation, 5) the careful balancing of the level of the Dead sea in order to accommodate introduction of either Mediterranean or Red sea water for HE and RO production, 6) the necessity of a combination of short-term, medium-term, and long-term responses to growing water shortages, 7) the need for long range planning to begin now, and 8) emphasis on cooperative regional development.

We do not present this study as the answer to the problems of supplying water to the core area. We hope only that our thoughts will stimulate others to seek the best possible comprehensive answer to the long-term hydrologic needs of the region. In this way peace can be achieved and reinforced.

We see the problems encountered, the negotiations attempted, and the resulting answers, as having worldwide application. Though the Middle East and the Mashreq are unique in many ways, they are also paradigms for the American south-west, the rivers of farther Asia, and even the more copious flows of Europe and the higher latitudes. This can be illustrated by a poet's perception of the future.

The American poet Carl Sandburg tells in a short verse how one night he was travelling on a train hurtling across the prairie. As he sat there staring into the dark, he mused on how in a hundred years all the train's passengers would be dust and the train itself an abandoned hulk or its metal recast into some other mode. He turned to a fellow passenger and asked him where he was going, and the passenger replied, 'to Kansas city'.

The locale we have discussed may be the Middle East rather than the Middle West, but all of us, the present authors and the audience whom they address, are like passengers on some train rushing through the dark to an obscure future. And yet, the painful process by means of which peace is being wrought in the Middle East is a positive one, applicable throughout the world. That this is so seems more possible today then even a scant decade ago. Such muted optimism is certainly possible when considering the role of water in the ongoing peace process. As described above, negotiations have progressed, new approaches to water acquisition and equitable sharing are under active discussion, and technological solutions to the growing water shortage are being studied and some are already being put in place.

Finally, we realize that our relationship to all natural sources of water, be they rivers, aquifers, or oceans is a truly symbiotic one. That if those sources suffer, so will we. We must learn to think holistically, from source to sea, and extend the time frame of our perceptions to spans of years and decades, to future droughts and surpluses and burgeoning populations. We must see the sources of water as living entities and become their advocates, so that all peoples may prosper in a healthy and sustainable environment.

Bibliography
(* Environmental Studies)

Abu-Zeid, M. A. and Rady M.A. 1991. 'Egypt's Water Resources Management and Policies', Comprehensive Water Resources Management Policy Workshop, World Bank, Washington, D.C., June 24–8.

Ascher, W. 1989. 'Limits of Expert Systems' for Political-Economic Forecasting. *Technological Forecasting and Social Change*, 36.

Assaf, Karen, Nader al Khatib, Elisha Kally, Hillel Shuval. 1993. *A Proposal for the Development of a Regional Water Master Plan*, (Israel/Palestine Center for Research and Information, Jerusalem), p. ix & 192.

Bakour, Yahia. May, 1991. 'Planning and Management of Water Resources in Syria', Arab Organization for Agricultural Development, Damascus Regional Office.

Bakour, Yahia, and John Kolars. 1994. 'The Arab Mashreq — Hydrologic History, Problems and Perspectives,' In: *Water in the Arab World — Perspectives and Prognoses*, Peter Rogers and Peter Lydon (eds), Cambridge, Harvard University Press, 121–45.

*Barth, Hans-Gunter, Aysel Bayraktar, Dorgan Kantarci, Gunay Kocasoy, Aysen Muezzinoglu. 1987. CED (Cevresel Etki Degerlendirme) Uygulamasindan Ornekler/ Examples of the Application of Improving Impact on the Environment (Turkiye Cevre Sorunlari Vakfi: Ankara) p. 187.

Baskin, Gershon. Summer, 1994. 'The Clash Over Water: an Attempt at Demystification', *Palestine-Israel Journal of Politics, Economics and Culture*, No. 3: 27–35.

Beatley, Timothy, David J. Brower, Anna K. Schwab. 1994. *An Introduction to Coastal Zone Management*, Island Press, Washington, DC. p. xi & 210.

*Beaumont, Peter, *Environmental Management and Development in Dry Lands* Routledge, London and New York, 1989, xix and 505.

————, 'The Myth of Water Wars and the Future of Irrigated Agriculture in the Middle East,' *International Journal of Water Resource Development*, Vol. 10, no. 1, 1994, 9-21.

*Biswas, Asit K., 'Environmental Sustainability of Egyptian Agriculture: Problems and Perspective,' *Ambio*, Vol. 24, No. 1, February, 1995, 16-20.

*————, 'Objectives and Concepts of environmentally-sound Water Management,' *Environmentally Sound Water Management*, N.C. Thanh and Asit K. Biswas, (eds.), Oxford University Press, Delhi, 1990, 30-58.

*————, 'Watershed Management', *Environmentally Sound Water Management*, N.C. Thanh and Asit K. Biswas, (eds.), (Oxford University Press, Delhi, 1990, 155-175.

————, 'Shared Natural Resources: Source of Conflict or Springs of Peace?', *Development Forum*, v. 13 1982.

Biswas, A.K., Kolars, J., Wolf, A.T., Murakami, M. etc., *International Water Issues of the Middle East: from Tigris-Euphrates to Nile,* United Nations University (UNU) and International Water Resources Association (IWRA), Oxford University Press, 1994, 117-155.

Biswas, A.K., *et al*, *Water For Sustainable Development in the 21st Century*, A.K. Biswas, M. Jellali, G. Stout, (eds.), Oxford University Press, Delhi 1993, xvi & 272.

*Bowden, Charles, *Killing the Hidden Waters—The Slow Destruction of Water Resources in the American Southwest*, University of Texas Press, Austin: 1977, 174.

Calder I.R. and Neal C., 'Evaporation from Saline Lakes: A Combination Equation Approach', *IAHS Journal of Hydrological Science*, Vol. 29, No. 1, 1984, 89-97.

Carbone, Gregory J. 'Issues of Spatial and Temporal Variability in Climate Impact Studies', *The Professional Geographer*, Vol. 47, No. 1, February 1995, 30-40.

Collins, Robert, *The Waters of the Nile*, Oxford University Press, New York, 1990.

Congressional Quarterly Almanac, '90th Congress', 1st Session, 1967.

Coplin, W. and M. O'Leary, *Everyman's Prince: A Guide to Understanding Your Political Problems*, New York, Dusbury Press, 1976.

————. 1983. *Political Analysis through the PRINCE System.* Policy Studies Association, New York.

Cotillon, J., 1993. *Water from Dams in Syria,* International Commission on Large Dams, Paris, p. 56.

Cran, James A. 1994. 'Medusa Bag Projects for the Ocean transport of freshwater in the Mediterranean and Middle East,' A paper presented at the VIII World Water Congress, Cairo, November 21, p. 6.

David, G., 1991. 'The Setting of the Peace Pipeline', MEED, 26 March 1988, p. 10.

Davis, Uri, Antonia Maks, John Richardson. 1980. 'Israel's Water Policies', *Journal of Palestine Studies* 9 (2; 34): 3–32.

Delli Priscoli, Jerome. 1992. 'Collaboration, Participation and Alternative Dispute Resolution (ADR): Process Concepts for the Bank's Role in Water Resources', prepared for the World Bank November 1992.

Deming, David. 1995. 'Climatic Warming in North America: Analysis of Borehole Temperatures,' *Science* **268**: 1576–77.

Dinar, A. and A. Wolf. October 1994. 'International Markets for Water and the Potential for Regional Cooperation: Economic and Political Perspectives in the Western Middle East,' *Economic Development and Cultural Change* **43** (1): 43–66.

*Dynesius, Mats and Christopher Nilsson. 1994. 'Fragmentation and Flow Regulation of River systems in the Northern Third of the World,' *Science* **266**, 4 Nov: 753–62.

Elmusa, Sharif S. 1994. 'Rethinking Water—Water may not be the catalyst for war or peace Everyone Thinks It is', *Middle East Insight* **XI** (1) November-December: 35–7.

————. 1994. 'The Israeli-Palestinian Water Dispute can be Solved,' *Palestine-Israel Journal of Politics, Economics and Culture*, No 3, Summer: 18–26.

Falkenmark, Malin, Lundqvist, J., and Widstrand, C. 1989. 'Macro-Scale Water Scarcity Requires Micro-Scale Approaches. Aspects of Vulnerability in Semi-Arid Development', *Natural Resources Forum* **13** (4): 258–67.

Frey, Frederick. 1992. 'The Political Context of Conflict and Cooperation over International River Basins,' Conference on the Middle East Water Crisis, Waterloo, Canada, May 7-9.

Galnoor, Itzhak. 1978. 'Water Policy Making in Israel', *Policy Analysis* 4: 339–67.

Garber, Andra, and Elias Salameh, (eds.) 1992. *Jordan's Water Resources and Their Future Potential*, Amman, Siftung.

Gershon, Baskin. Summer 1994. 'The Clash Over Water: an Attempt at Demystification' *Palestine-Israel Journal of Politics, Economics and Culture*, No 3: 27–35.

Gleick, Peter H. April, 1994. 'Water, War & Peace in the Middle East', *Environment*, p. 6–15 and p. 35–41.

Glueckstern, P. 1982. 'Preliminary Consideration of Combining A Large Reverse Osmosis Plant with the Mediterranean-Dead Sea Project,' *Desalination* 40: 143–56.

Gonzalez, Arturo and Santiago Rubio. 1992. 'Optimal Interbasin Water Transfers in Spain', In: *Sharing Scarce Freshwater Resources in the Mediterranean Basin: An Economic Perspective*, Padova, Italy, April 23–4.

Gordon, T. and O. Helmer. 1964. 'Report on a Long Range Forecasting Study'. Santa Monica (CA): RAND Corporation.

*Goudie, Andrew and John Wilkinson. 1977. *The Warm Desert Environment*, Cambridge University Press, Cambridge. p. 88.

Gurr, Ted. 1985. 'On the Political Consequences of Scarcity and Economic Decline', *International Studies Quarterly* 29: 51–75.

Hazell, Peter, et al., 1994. 'Effects of Deregulation of the Agricultural Production Sector on Food Availability and Resource Use in Egypt', IFPRI Washington, DC.

Hillel, Daniel. 1994. *Rivers of Eden*, Oxford University Press, New York, p. xii and 355.

Howe, C. and Easter K. 1971. *Interurban Transfers of Water: Economic Issues and Impacts*, Johns Hopkins University Press, Baltimore.

Inbar, Moshe and Jacob Maos. 1984. 'Water Resource Planning and Development in the Northern Jordan Valley', *Water International* 9: 18–25.

International Law Assocation. 1967. *Report of the Fifty-second conference*, Helsinki (London: ILA).

International Law Commission. 1979. *First Report on the Law of Non-navigational Use of International Water Course*, submitted to UN General Assembly (New York, UNGE, 79–61671).

———. 1991. *Report of the ILC on the Work of Its Forty-third Session*, UN General Assembly Supplement No. 10 (A/46/10), New York.

ISPAN. 1994. *Integrated Planning for Sustainable Use of Water in the Middle East,* Irrigation Support Project for Asia and the Near East, Arlington, USA, p. viii and 73.

————, *Resolving Water disputes—Conflict and Cooperation in the United States, the Near East, and Asia,* Irrigation Support Project for Asia and the Near East, Arlington, USA, p. x and 156.

*————. 1992. *Gulf of Aqaba Environmental Data Survey, see* Peter Reisse, et al.

Israel (State). 1992. Central Bureau of Statistics, *Statistical Abstract of Israel,* No. 43: 426–59.

Israel/PLO. 1993. 'Text of Declaration of Principles', Annex-IV, *Jerusalem Post,* September 15.

Israel/Palestine Center for Research and Information. 1993. *Water: Conflict or Cooperation,* (ed.), G. Baskin, Vol II of *Israel/Palestine Issues in Conflict—Issues for Cooperation,* Number 2, March p. 114.

*Issar, Arie S. 1995. 'Climatic Change and the History of the Middle East', *American Scientist* 83 (4), July–August: 350–55.

JVA (Jordan Valley Authority). 1981. 'Potential for the Development of Hydropower between the Red Sea and Dead Sea', Harza Overseas Engineering Co., Ltd., Main Report.

Khaldi, Nabil. 1992. 'The Emergence of Barley in the Middle East and North Africa: the Case of Syria,' IFPRI, Washington, DC.

Kally, Elisha and Avraham Tal. 1989. 'A Middle East Water Plan under Peace' in Meir Mehav (ed.) *Economic Cooperation and Middle East Peace, Weidenfeld and Nicolson,* London. 48–116.

Kepner, C. and Tregoe B. 1965. *The Rational Manager,* McGraw-Hill New York.

*Kerr, Richard A. 1995. 'Studies say—Tentatively—that Greenhouse Warming is Here,' *Science* 268, 16 June 1995, 1567–8.

Kliot, Nurit. 1994. *Water Resources and Conflict in the Middle East,* Routlege, London .p. xv and 309.

*Kolars, John. 1994. 'Managing the Impact of Development: The Euphrates and Tigris Rivers and the Ecology of the Arabian Gulf—A Link in Forging Tri-Riparian Cooperation,' *Water as an Element of Cooperation and Development in the Middle East,* Ali Ihsan Bagis, (ed.), Ayna Publications and the Friedrich Naumann Foundation in Turkey, Ankara. p. 129–54.

————. 1993. 'The Litani River in the Context of Middle Eastern

Water Resources,' *Prospects for Lebanon*, Centre for Lebanese Studies Oxford. p. 21–60 and 3.

————.'1993. The Middle East's Growing Water Crisis', *Research and Exploration*, National Geographic Society, Special Issue: 'Water-Reflections on an Elusive Resource' 9 November 1993, p. 38–49.

————.1992a. 'Les Resources en eau du Liban—Le Litani dans son cadre regional', *monde arabe—Maghreb-Machrek*, No. 138, Oct/Dec., 11–26.

————. 1992b. 'The Future of the Euphrates River', *Country Experiences with Water Resources Management: Economic, Institutional, Technological and Environmental Issues*, World Bank Technical Publication 175, Guy LeMoigne, (ed.), World Bank, Washington, DC. 135–42.

————.'1992c. Water Resources of the Middle East', *Canadian Journal of Development*, Special Issue, *Sustainable Water Resources Management in Arid Countries*. p. 103–19.

Kolars, John F. and William A. Mitchell. 1991. *The Euphrates River and the Southeast Anatolia Development Project*, Southern Illinois University Press, Carbondale. p. xxix and 324.

Kubursi, A. A., and Amery H. A. 1992. The Litani and the ebrith of Lebanon', paper delivered at the *Conference on the Middle East Water Crisis*, Waterloo, Ontario, May 7–9.

Lekakis, Joseph, and Dimitrios Giannias. 1991. 'Optimal Freshwater Allocation: The Case of Nestos', in draft.

Linstone, H. and M. Turoff (eds.). 1975. *The Delphi Method: Techniques and Applications*,Addison-Wesle Reading, USA.

Lowi, Miriam. 1993. Water and Power: *The Politics of a Scarce Resource in the Jordan River Basin*, Cambridge University Press, Cambridge.

Mar'ai, Sayyid al- and Saad Hagras. 1975. *If the Arabs Want It*, Dar al- Ta'awan, Cairo (in Arabic).

Maw'ad, Hamad Sa'id al. 1993. *Water Wars in the Middle East*, Dar Kana'an li Dirasat wa Nashr, Damascus n.d. (in arabic).

Mediterranean-Dead Sea Co., Ltd. 1983. 'Mediterranean-Dead Sea Project' Outline Design—Summary and Conclusions.

Meedham, R. and de Loë R. 1990. 'The Policy Delphi: Purpose, Structure, and Application'. *The Canadian Geographer* 32 (2).

Michael, M. 1974. 'The Allocation of Waters of International Rivers', *Natural Resources Lawyer*, **9** (1), p. 45–66.

Mikhail, Wakil. 1992. 'Analysis of Future Water Needs for Different Sectors in Syria', Conference on the Middle East Water Crisis, Waterloo, Canada, May 7–9.

Moore, James H. 1992. 'Water-Sharing Regimes in Israel and the Occupied Terriotories—A Technical Analysis', Department of National Defense, Ottowa Canada.

Moore, James H. 1994. 'Parting the Waters: Calculating Israeli and Palestinian Entitlements to the West Bank Aquifers and the Jordan River Basin', *Middle East Policy*, III (2): 91–1108.

Murakami, M. 1995. *Managing Water for Peace in the Middle East— Alternative Strategies*, United Nations University Press, Tokyo.

————. 1994. 'Non-conventional Water Resources Development Alternatives to Satisfy Water Demand in the 21st Century', Proceedings of the VIII IWRA World Congress on Water Resources, Vol. I, National Water Research Center, Ministry of Public Works and Water resources, Cairo, Nov. 1994, (T5-S1) 21–19.

————. 1993a. 'Hydro-powered Reverse Osmosis (RO) Desalination for Cogeneration : A Middle East Case Study,' Proceedings of the IDA and WRPC World Congress on Desalination and Water Treatment , Vol. II, 37–44.

————. 1993b. 'Water for Peace Master Plan of the Jordan River System,' Proceedings of the IDA and WRPC World Congress on Desalination and Water Treatment: Vol. II, 621–29.

————. 1991. 'Arid Zone Water Resources Planning Study with Applications of Non-conventional Alternatives.' Doctoral thesis, University of Tokyo, Japan.

Murakami, M. and Wolf, A. 1995. 'A Middle East Techno-political Water Resources Development Alternatives for the Dead Sea and Aqaba Regions,' *International Journal of Water Resources Development* 11 (2): 147–62.

Naff, Thomas and Ruth C. Matson. 1984. *Water in the Middle East—Conflict or Cooperation?* Westview Press, Boulder and London, p. 236.

*Naiman, Robert J., *et al*. 1995. 'Freshwater Ecosystems and Their Management: A National Initiative', *Science* **270** 27 October, p. 584–5.

Oak Ridge National Laboratory. 1970. 'Middle East Study Application of Large Water-Producing Energy Centers: Gaza Area Development and Refugee Resettlement,' Draft, November 10.

O.C.D.E. 1985. *Management of Water Projects: Decision-Making and Investment Appraisal,* Paris: 1985,p. 2254.

Omran, Abdel and Farzaneh Roudi. 1993. *The Middle East Population Puzzle, Population Bulletin,* Population Reference Bureau, Inc., 48 (1): July, p. 40.

Palestine-Israel Journal of Politics, Economics and Culture. 1994. No author given, 'Focus on Water, Water in the Israeli-Arab Conflict', 'Introduction.' No. 3, 11–17.

Rizaiza, Omar S. Abu and Mohamed N. Allam. 1989. 'Water Requirements versus Water Availability in Saudi Arabia', *Journal of Water Resources Planning and Management* 115 (1): January, p. 64–74.

Richards, Alan. 1994. 'The Impact of Structural Adjsutment on Agricultural Development in the Near East Region', FAO Economic and Social Policy Pager, draft in April.

Rogers, Peter. 1991. 'International River Basins: Pervasive Unidirectional Externalities', paper presented the conference 'The Economics of Transnational Commons,' Universita di Siena, Italy April 25–27.

Rogers, Peter and Peter Lydon (eds.) 1994. *Water in the Arab World* Harvard University Press, Cambridge, p. xix and 369.

Ross, P. 1983. 'Med-Dead Canal: New Life for an Old Idea', *Barron's* December 5.

Salameh, Elias and Helen Bannayan. 1993. *Water Resources of Jordan— Present Status and Future Potentials,* Friedrich Ebert Siftung and Royal Society for the Conservation of Nature, Amman, p. iv & 183.

Starr, Joyce. 1991. 'Water Wars', *Foreign Policy,* Number 82, Spring, 17–36,

Stern, E. and Gradus Y. 1981. 'The Med-Dead Sea Project—A Vision or Reality?', 12 *Geoforum* 3, 268.

Strauss, L. 1967. 'Dwight Eisenhower's 'Proposal for Our Time', *National Review,* V. 37, 1008.

Tahal Israel. 1982. 'MDS Project', Project Summary in Feasibility Study Report, 1982.

*Tenenbaum, David. 1994. 'Rethinking the River', *Nature Conservancy,* July/August, p. 11–15.

Thanh, N.C. and Tam D.M. 1990. 'Water systems and the Environment', N.C. Thanh and Asit K. Biswas, *Environmentally Sound Water Management,* Oxford University Press, Delhi, p. 1–29.

*Uhir, P. F. and Carter G.C. 1994. *Crop Modeling and Related Enviromental Data—a Focus on Applications for Arid and Semi-arid Regions in Developing Countries,* CODATA Commission on Global Change Data, CODATA Monograph Series, Vol. 1, CODATA, 51 Boulevard de Montmorency, 75016 Paris.

United Nations. 1990. *World Urbanization Prospects—*1990, Department of International Economic and Social Affairs, United Nations, New York City.

*United Scientists for Projects and Development & High Institute of Public Health—Alexandria University. 1991. Proceeding of *International Symposium on Environmental Protection is a Must (sic)* Alexandria, Egypt, 11–14 March. p. 513.

*US National Science Foundation and National Research Council, *Selected Papers from Workshop on Natural Disasters in European Mediterranean Countries,* Columbella, Perugia, Italy. 27 June–1 July, p. 488.

US Water News. 1995. 'China is going ahead with construction of Three Gorges Dam,' **11** (9) March,p. 2.

———. 1995. Editorial, 'Population growth will have major impact on water resources,' **11** (11) May, p. 6.

*Van Dyke, Jon M., Durwood Zaelke, Grant Hewison, (eds.). 1993. *Freedom for the Seas in the Twenty-first Century—Ocean Governance and Environmental Harmony,* Island Press, p. 430.

Waterbury, John. 1979. *Hydropolitics of the Nile Valley,* Syracuse University Press.

———. 1994. 'Transboundary Water and the Challenge of International Cooperation in the Middle East', *Water in the Arab world— Perspectives and Prognoses,* Peter Rogers and Peter Lydon (eds.) Division of Applied Sciences, Harvard University Cambridge, p. 1–37.

Wishart, David. 1990. 'The Breakdown of the Johnston Negotiations over the Jordan Waters,' *Middle Eastern Studies* 26 (4) p. 45–53.

Wolf, Aaron. 1994. *Hydropolitics Along the Jordan River: The Impact of Scarce Water Resources on the Arab-Israeli Conflict,* United Nations University Press, Tokyo.

————. 1993. 'Water for Peace in the Jordan River Watershed', *Natural Resources Journal* 33 (3) Summer, 797–839.

————. 1992. 'The Impact of Scarce Water Resources on the Arab-Israeli Conflict: An Interdisciplinary Study of Water Conflict Analysis and Proposal for Conflict Resolution', The University of Wisconsin-Madison.

World Bank. 1993. *A Strategy for Managing Water in the Middle East and North Africa*, Washington, DC.

————. 1988. 'Jordan Water Resources Sector Study', World Bank Report No.7099-JO, 1–38.

WPDC (Water Power and Dam Construction). 1983. 'Jordan Attacks Dead Sea Project,' *International News*, March, p. 4.

————. 1989. 'Dead Sea P-S Scheme Revived', *World News*, May 1, p. 3.

Zayyati, Nu'man al. 1994. 'The Nile: The Struggle Explodes among Neighbors', *al-Ahram al-Iqtisadi*, July 4, 12–15 (in arabic).

Zeitouni, Naomi, Nir Becker, and Mordechai Shecter. 1992. 'Trading in Water Rights in an International Context: The Mediterranean Arena', Draft copy.

Index